Temperance Facts

By. W.G. Calderwood

Temperance Facts
By. W.G. Calderwood

Edited, With an Introduction, by
Jonathan T. Makeley

Whitlock Publishing
Alfred, New York

Original published by the Minnesota Temperance Movement 1940

First Whitlock Publishing Edition 2017

Editorial Matter © Jonathan T. Makeley

ISBN: 978-1-943115-22-8

Table of Contents

History   117

Introduction

Following the end of Prohibition, as its history was fading away from public conception into the fog of mythos, a man set forth to counteract this and set the record straight. In 1940, W.G. (Willis Greenleaf) Calderwood wrote the concise informational book *Temperance Facts*. This seasoned temperance activist and Prohibition Party politician, who had been one of the architects of national prohibition, compiled a set of factual information to make his case that the national prohibition of alcohol had been a successful policy that had been undermined by elite interests, that repeal was a mistake, and that it would be better to reestablish Prohibition.

In doing so, he produced a work which offers a variety of insights and considerations . It offers historical and factual information, as well as pro-prohibition interpretation of them. It illuminates aspects of the Wet efforts to undermine prohibition, and to create a mythos against it, which to this day heavily influences common conceptions about the period of national prohibition. It touches on matters of history, inviting the need for a critical consideration of common beliefs, and the importance of checking the public view against historical and factual evidence. The implications of it can offer insights into modern day debates on how to address alcohol and other intoxicants, as well for longstanding themes of reformist efforts, and the matters of the use of the state to combat social ills.

Life of W.G. Calderwood

W.G. Calderwood was born July 25th, 1866, in Fox Lake, Wisconsin. He was the son of a Wesleyan Methodist minister and spent his childhood in Wisconsin and Iowa. As a teenager, he worked to support himself and to afford an education. At the age of sixteen, he entered the Wesleyan Methodist Seminary at Wasioja, graduating in 1886. He attended college in Chicago and graduated in 1890.[1] He then set out to build his life in Minneapolis, Minnesota. In 1889, he began teaching at the American Commercial College in Minneapolis, and began his association with the Prohibition Party. In 1892, he married his wife Alice M. Cox (who was likewise the child of a Wesleyan Methodist preacher and was said to have shared an intertest in her husband's endeavors). He worked as a college teacher until 1903, when he started his employment with the Northwestern Life Insurance Company. He eventually moved into a full-time commitment to politics, writing, and community involvement.[2]

Temperance and Prohibitionist politics would end up being Calderwood's main field of activism. Through the course of his political involvement, Calderwood rose to become a leading figure in the party. In 1897, he became executive secretary of the Minnesota State Prohibition Party Committee. In 1902, he goes before the state committee with a report on his investigations into public sentiment, and makes the case that they were in the position to mount serious campaigns to win elected office in the state. Their efforts end up being highly successful. The party's vote in the state rose from 4,000 in 1902 to 53,000 in 1910, and they began regularly electing multiple members of the state legislature.[3]

He used his familiarity with the law to stand up against alcohol interests. In 1909, he filed several lawsuits against brewing companies and the city of Minneapolis, in order to make them return the refunds that Minneapolis had given for canceling their liquor licenses.[4] In 1910, he responded to the problem of settlers selling alcohol in areas of Northern Minnesota which were prohibited by a treaty with the Chippewa. His research and legal advocacy on the matter pushed the Interior Department's chief special agent on Indian Affairs, William Johnson, to issue an order closing all saloons in the treaty area.[5]

Calderwood came to acquire leading positions within the party. In 1905, he became secretary of the National Prohibition Committee, and would hold the position until 1914. In 1910, he became the state chairman in Minnesota, and holds the position until 1920.[6] In the 1912 Prohibition Party National Convention, Calderwood was a major contender for the Chairman position. He was supported by the so-called "insurgent" element of the party against former Chairman Charles Jones (who was supported by the "Conservative Wing" of the party). In the end, Virgil Hinshaw was selected as a compromise between the factions as the new Chairman.[7] Though Calderwood did not get to be chairman, he did become a member of the party's national executive committee.[8] In the 1916 convention, received 22 delegate votes and came in fourth place in the selection for the Prohibition Party Candidate for President.[9]

Though while he was helping to lead and build the Prohibition Party, he also ran for public office several times. In 1904, he ran for 39th district Minnesota State House; receiving 1067 votes and 9.54% of the vote. In 1912, he ran as the Prohibition candidate for Minnesota Congressman At Large; receiving 25,824 votes and 9.24% of the vote. In1914, he ran for Governor of Minnesota; receiving 18,582 votes and 5.41% of the vote. In 1916, he ran as the Prohibition Party candidate for U.S. senate; receiving 78,425 votes and 20.58% of the vote. In

1918, he ran for senate again; this time on the National Party ticket. The National Party was a short-lived coalition of Pro-war socialists, Prohibitionists, Suffragists, Progressives, and the like. This time, he received 137,334 votes, 39.95% of the vote and came in second place.[10]

He also turned his campaign skills toward helping other Prohibition Party candidates. In 1914, he became the campaign manager for Charles Randell's congressional campaign. Randell's campaign succeeded and he became the first Prohibition Party candidate elected to the U.S. Congress.[11]

The Prohibitionist movement gained strength in the 1910's. After the 1916 election, congress passed the bill for the 18th Amendment, which would be ratified a few years later after enough states adopted the amendment. The prohibitionist tide was further accelerated by United States' entry into World War I. In 1917, a committee was formed by the government, to consider establishing wartime restriction on the manufacture of alcohol as a means of saving grains for the war effort.[12] Calderwood acted as the executive secretary of the committee, and by July of that year called for the establishment of wartime prohibition.[13] Congress passed the Wartime Prohibition Act in 1918. In 1919, the 18th Amendment was ratified, and the Volstead Act (the law setting federal policies for enforcing the 18th Amendment) was passed.[14]

After National Prohibition had started, Calderwood continued to promote the prohibitionist cause. In 1920, he unsuccessfully tried to get William Jennings Bryan and Billy Sunday to run as the Prohibition Party's presidential ticket.[15] Bryan was a populist Democratic politician and former secretary of state, who was known for supporting the silver standard, prohibition, anti-imperialism, and trust busting.[16] Rev. Billy Sunday was a former professional baseball player and a famous evangelical minister, who was well known as an advocate for Prohibition.[17]

Subsequently, Calderwood turned toward promoting prohibition internationally. From 1921-1923, he embarked on a campaign in Australia to help groups campaigning for prohibition in that country.[18] He would later go on a second campaign in Australia in 1939-40.[19] Throughout the period of national prohibition, he wrote numerous articles and letters to newspapers, arguing in favor of the successes of National Prohibition and arguing against attacks on it, by anti-prohibitionist (aka Wet) critics.

As the political threats against National Prohibition grew larger, Calderwood grew more fervent in his efforts to counter Wet propaganda. In 1932, he became the head of the newly formed *Prohibition Facts* Service. It was a national organization, headquartered in Minneapolis, with the declared mission of providing factual information to counter false claims by anti-prohibitionists about Prohibition and the effects of repeal.[20] This lead him to begin producing his *Prohibition Facts* book series, between 1932-35. After National Prohibition was repealed in 1933, and once there was data on the effect of repeal to compare National Prohibition with, he decided he was in place to write another book. This was further motivated by concern that Wet Propaganda may gain dominance over the public imagination. This led him, in 1940, to write *Temperance Facts*.

Calderwood continued to live for another 16 years, and passed on in 1956.[21]

Writings

The writing of *Temperance Facts* was the last significant product of his many years as a writer. Over the course of his life, W. G. Calderwood had engaged in an assortment of activist writing. These writings were often related to temperance, prohibition, and to broader political issues.

In 1909, he wrote his first book, *A. Lincoln: Reformer: Born February 12, 1809*. The book is on history of

Abraham Lincoln. It focuses on painting a picture of Lincoln's political philosophy and his work as a reformist. Lincoln was a religiously devout person, who believed in the moral improvement of society, supported prohibition, and had boldly acted for what was right. Calderwood was a fan of Abraham Lincoln. He promoted a positive memorial of Lincoln, and interpreted him in ways that paralleled him with his own cause.[22] In other writings, Calderwood argued that the Prohibition Party was the true inheritor the founding fathers and Lincoln, and that the Prohibition movement was the natural continuance of their legacy.[23]

Calderwood authored a number of essays on Prohibition and the Prohibition Party. For instance, in 1908, he wrote "Prohibition as A Present Political Platform". In this he argues that Prohibition is worthy of being the center of a political platform on the basis that it is an issue which concerns the fundamental principles of government, is of a magnitude of significant importance, and is an unsettled issue capable of being settled.[24] In other essays, he had written on the social, economic, and human costs of the alcohol industry to make the case the industry should be eliminated. He made philosophical arguments on how the legality of alcohol was contrary to moral and national principles, and against those who tried to claim a personal liberty to alcohol.[25]

During the period of National Prohibition, he wrote a series of articles and letters to newspapers. These were often written in response to anti-prohibitionist claims. Such as pointing out that a Wet figure who gave a report claiming increased illegal alcohol production under prohibition had misrepresented and fabricated data.[26] In other articles, he challenged the claims of increased tax revenue and economic activity from legalizing alcohol. [27]He often used his wit in his articles to counter his opponents. In one article, he gives a satirical argument, taking Wet arguments about the dynamics of law and social behavior, applying them to the issue of murder, and stating by that logic that you could reduce murder by making it legal to stab and shoot people.[28] Over the course of his various writings, one can see the themes emerging of the issues that Calderwood would tackle in *Temperance Facts*.

In 1932, Calderwood began writing books on National Prohibition. In 1932, he wrote the first of his *Prohibition Facts* books. This was followed by his second in 1933, and his third in 1935. The *Prohibition Facts* books are similar to *Temperance Facts* in much of its content and format. These books provided information to contend about the harms of alcohol and the benefits of prohibition. Themes and information used in these books ended up being reused and updated in *Temperance Facts*.[29] The second book's sectional organization seems out of the three books to be the one most similar to the organization in *Temperance Facts*.[30]

Though, with *Temperance Facts* there is a shift in tone, related to its different historical context. The first and second *Prohibition Facts* were written before the repeal of National Prohibition, and took a tone of urging resistance to repeal. The third book came shortly after prohibition (through too soon to get post-prohibition data), and drifted in a relatively more philosophic direction, with a sense that a new phase in temperance activity was beginning.[31]

Temperance Facts came out several years after the end of National Prohibition, and reflected a new intellectual formulation on political temperance. It endeavored to use information to contend that prohibition had been a successful policy and that repealing it had been a mistake. It hoped to use public education to persuade more of the public toward supporting Prohibitionism and toward trying to reinstate prohibition. The additional analysis of the forces involved in Wet propaganda and anti-prohibitionist organization, offered a means to assuring that possible future attempts against prohibition could be countered, and prohibition could attain a long term viability. *Temperance Facts*, in addition to being an informative work, was a culmination of much of his previous writing and a thesis for continuing Prohibitionism in Post-repeal America.[32]

Historical Context

This book is also part of a broader history of the Temperance and Prohibition movement in American history. In the beginning of the 19th century, a rising tide of reformism met an increased concern over the increasing alcohol problems which the nation was facing, and resulted in the creation of the Temperance movement.[33] Within a half century it developed into a mass movement, and the elements of teetotalism (total abstinence from the use of alcohol) and prohibitionism began to arise within it. Over the course of the 19th century, the popularity of teetotalism and prohibitionism worked to rise in prominence.[34] Prohibitionism tended to arise initially with efforts to ban alcohol in local communities, and grew to county and statewide efforts.[35] In the 1850's, Maine became the first state to practice statewide Prohibition, and was followed by several other states.[36] However, within a decade most of these state laws were either repealed or discarded by state courts.[37] This would lead prohibition supporters to engage in another period of building support, and encouraged the determination that the success of prohibition efforts would be aided by Dry politicians and the constitutional enshrinement of prohibition.

The Prohibition Party was founded in 1869, by John Russel, James Black, and their associates. The initial membership of the Prohibition Party tended to consist of temperance activists, and other reform activists, such as supporters for women suffrage.[38] Plenty of prohibition supporters were former abolitionists, and or supporters of women's rights. It drew people who had become disaffected with Republican Party and wanted to push further for social reform. In addition to supporting prohibition, its early platforms included support for women's suffrage, equal pay for women, and advancing civil rights and racial equality. Over the decades, the party grew to become one of the major third party groups in the country.[39]

The Prohibition Party, the Women's Christian Temperance Union, the Anti Saloon League, and various other groups engaged in a concentrated effort to promote Prohibition. The 1880's had another wave of state level activity. Kansas led the pack and established a state level prohibition that lasted into National Prohibition. At their most effective, the Prohibition Party's presidential candidates drew hundreds of thousands of votes. After they helped throw the results of two elections against the Republicans, the major parties began to significantly get behind establishing national prohibition.[40]

The Prohibitionist movement gained strength in the 1910's. After the 1916 election, congress passed the bill for the 18th Amendment, which would be ratified a few years later after enough states adopted the amendment. This war further accelerated by United States' entry into World War I, which lead to the War Time Prohibition Act. In 1919, the 18th Amendment was ratified, and the Volstead act was passed.[41]

National Prohibition lasted for roughly 13 years. This period saw anti-prohibitionist efforts to repeal it. This eventually resulted in the passage of the 21st Amendment in 1933, repealing National Prohibition. [42] Though the end of National Prohibition did not mean the end of temperance and prohibitionism. Supporters, such Calderwood, continued to advocate for Prohibition after being returned to the status of a socio-political minority.

Post Repeal Prohibitionist Historical Arguments

Following the end of prohibition, Wets endeavored to define people's common notions of prohibition. They worked to try to convince people that prohibition had been a failure and to attribute various negative phenomena to it. This initially came as an outgrowth of the anti-prohibition propaganda which had occurred during national prohibition, and acted to try to secure the effort to bring it down. This included the repetitive use of fabricated statistics and reports, portraying crime, health problems, and social dysfunction to be more common than actually were, blaming prohibition for the drinking committed by people violating the law, giving disproportionate expression to the opponents and violators of national prohibition.[43] Over time, these efforts worked toward producing a public image against prohibition: one which would create a pervasive mythos that would replicate this belief in future generations and serve as a medium for attacking prohibitionist policies and social reform efforts. To a certain extent, these efforts have succeeded in creating a popular mythos about what many people generally think prohibition to have been.

This has not been met without resistance on the part of prohibitionists. Calderwood's *Temperance Facts* acted as an effort to resist wet efforts to dominate public thought on the matter. It sought to offer a counter argument that would be used to help influence the public and provide intellectual ammunition for those who continued to defend prohibition. But it also came to be an early part of efforts by prohibition supporters to comment on the history of prohibition, to argue that it was more successful than commonly portrayed, to challenge claims against prohibition which did not accord with historical facts, and to call for people to reconsider their beliefs about it.

The Prohibition Party has continued to bring forth people to make these historical arguments. Take for instance, the figure of the late Gene Amondson: minister, artist, temperance activist and 2008 Prohibition Party candidate for President. He was inspired to join the temperance cause after learning about Rev. Billy Sunday. He promoted the study of Billy Sunday and sought to bring more public attention to his sermon's and speeches on temperance. He worked to promote the prohibitionist cause, during his campaign and before, by pointing out the harms of alcohol and by putting forward information on the successes within the history of prohibition.[44]

The current Prohibition Party continues to make contentions about the history of National Prohibition. Jim Hedges, the Prohibition Party's 2016 candidate (who received the party's highest vote results since 1988) has undertaken efforts to inform people on the positive history of National Prohibition.[45] Various other members have drawn on historical information, including Calderwood's book, to contend for the viability of prohibition.

Members have also followed in the tradition of using contemporary information to formulate arguments for Prohibition. Georgia prohibitionist, Billy Joe Parker, has spent years visiting town halls and writing to newspapers, drawing on statistics such as the number of people annually killed by alcohol and the hundreds of thousands injured by alcohol related car accidents to encourage local governments and the state to adopt a new prohibition amendment.[46] In these and other instances, the techniques and efforts exemplified in Calderwood in *Temperance Facts* have continued.

Modern Relevance

This book also has relevance to issues in today's society, and perhaps may act in some way as an informative work. The understanding of the history National Prohi-

xviii   Introduction

bition helps inform some modern debates. Modern day
movements trying to legalize other intoxicants, such as
marijuana, often draw upon the popular notion of the
history of National Prohibition as a failure, to argue that
all prohibitive policies are negative and destined to fail.
Though Calderwood's account challenges this assumption. If it can be found that Calderwood's contentions are
in some sense correct than it undercuts their arguments.
In reflecting on Calderwood's account similarities can
be seen between the public messaging techniques of
the Wets and the modern legalizers. The comparison of
the Dry-Wet debate to modern day debates on the prohibition of other intoxicants, could be used a means for
analyzing these contemporary debates. Likewise, the
analysis of the historical contrasts between National
Prohibition and the Modern Drug War, serve to decon-
struct the wet-legalizer narrative.

The consideration of this book and the history of National Prohibition is also more proudly relevant to issues
of social reform efforts. Any movement which endeavors
to reform a major aspect of society, whether it be abo-
litionism and temperance, the civil rights movement,
the contemporary free college movement, must confront
the matter of mass persuasion in the face of opposing
interests, must endeavor exploring the possibilities and
challenges which come with endeavoring to create a new
human condition and social order, and explore how far
certain efforts are able to be affectual in the parameters
of their historical contexts.

Furthermore, *Temperance Facts* helps bring to consideration the matter of our own popular and historical
notions of things. How much do our popular notions re-
semble or deviate from historical fact? How accurate is
the information were are being provided on a matter?
How much of our popular notions are a product of propaganda? How much can we trust media to provide us

with accurate information? How can long-held popular beliefs, including ones that are often uncritical thinking, be uprooted? How, if we are aware of an inaccurate portrayal, do we then go about trying to remedy it and inform people? How can we endeavor to produce a thoughtful and accurately informed public? These are questions we grapple with on many issues. While it is obvious that there are answers, the question is what they are. And the only way to near them is through thinking about them. In this, *Temperance Facts* can be useful to help facilitate this thinking and understanding.

---

1. Horace B. Hudson, A Half Century of Minneapolis, (Minneapolis: The Hudson Publishing Company, 1908), https://books.google.com/books?id=F2ZAAAAAYAAJ&pg=PA493&lpg=PA493&dq=willis+greenleaf+calderwood&source=bl&ots=NrjNiMG-pA&sig=LVMdNmTxwgYuyS209Gb-2D0TZ-sk&hl=en&sa=X&ei=pMCXVbaaEIT_-AHG00-rACA&ved=0CD4Q6AEwBzgK#v=onepage&q=willis%20greenleaf%20calderwood&f=false, 493-494

2. Hill, John Wesley. Twin City Methodism: Being a History of the Methodist Episcopal Church in Minneapolis and St. Paul Minn.. Ed. Minneapolis: Price Bros. Publishing Co., 1895. https://books.google.com/books?id=QoUVAAAAYAAJ&pg=PA116&lpg=PA116&dq=willis+g+calderwood+die&source=bl&ots=7VT2WmlaOF&sig=TqHuphbC1xv9SS0CT_cixwuOUI4&hl=en&ei=MpdXTazvGIGC8gbbvozQBw&sa=X&oi=book_result&ct=result&resnum=2&ved=0CBwQ6AEwAQ#v=onepage&q=calderwood&f=false, 116-117; Who's who in Illinois, a biographical dictionary of leading men and women of the commonwealth, Vol. one, (Chicago: Larkin, Roosevelt, and Larkin LTD., 1947), Digitalized by the University of Illinois Internet Archive, 2012. https://archive.org/stream/whoswhoinillinoi00chic#page/n3/mode/2up, 1045;

Hudson, A Half Century of Minneapolis, 493-494; Who's who in America, Volume 9, Ed. John William Leonard and Albert Nelson Marquis, (Chicago: A. N. Marquis and Company, 1916), https://books.google.com/books?id=OlIlodoIyTkC&pg=PA376&lpg=PA376&dq=willis+greenleaf+calderwood&source=bl&ots=jUHNnd-NR1&sig=RpTXEinG-qR2AfMriyZ16IajxTY&hl=en&sa=X&ei=X9CXVYOlEYWu-QGfzb6ABA&ved=0CCwQ6AEwADgU#v=onepage&q=willis%20greenleaf%20calderwood&f=false, 376

3.   Hudson, A Half Century of Minneapolis, 493-494; American Prohibition Yearbook 1915, Ed. John A. Shields, (Chicago: Prohibition National Committee, 1915), https://books.google.com/books?id=22RDAQAAMAAJ&pg=PA20&lpg=PA20&dq=a+-maker+of+men+by+w.g.+calderwood&source=bl&ots=sBX6rfev6Y&sig=a8p-FFYvWY2_RF7fBRZV2jiHY_E&hl=en&sa=X-&ei=tJGVVfaFNIPo-QGc4bS4Dg&ved=0CC4Q6AEwBg#v=onepage&q=%20w.g.%20calderwood&f=false, 20-25; American Advance, (Chicago: Prohibition National Committee, 1911), https://books.google.com/books?id=XTniAAAAMAAJ&source=gbs_navlinks_s, 470; George M. Hammell, The Passing of the Saloon: An Authentic and Official Presentation of the Anti-Liquor Crusade in America, (Cincinnati: The Tower Press, 1908), https://books.google.com/books?hl=en&lr=&id=q1zlAAAAMAAJ&oi=fnd&pg=PR11&dq=w.g.+calderwood&ots=vwHIuTnz2G&sig=kEzBPcgSTWlrdlFIW_-OxOI5H8A#v=onepage&q=w.g.%20calderwood&f=false, 261

4.   City of Minneapolis, Annual Reports of the Various City Officers of the City of Minneapolis Minnesota For The Year 1909, (Minneapolis: Syndicate Printing Company, 1910), https://books.google.com/books?id=6KEaAQAAMAAJ&pg=RA1-PR68&lpg=RA1-PR68&dq=w.g.+calderwood&source=bl&ots=IehLoEMJ3K&sig=Gw5hVdwF2FMYo3mApvuko2KWZbM&hl=en&sa=X&ei=ER-UVZjLGMnksAWzxYj4BQ&ved=-0CEUQ6AEwCA#v=snippet&q=brewing&f=false, 7D-8D

5.   Kathryn A. Abbott, "Liquor law in Minnesota Indian coun-

try in the early twentieth century", Legal Studies Forum 25, no. 3/4 (January 2, 2001): 567-585, OmniFile Full Text Select (H.W. Wilson), EBSCOhost (accessed July 3, 2016), 567-585; Kathryn A. Abbott, "Alcohol and the Anishinaabeg of Minnesota in the Early Twentieth Century", The Western Historical Quarterly 30, no. 1 (1999): 25-43, http://ezproxy.alfred. edu:2122/stable/971157?Search=yes&resultItemClick=true&-searchText=calderwood&searchUri=%2Faction%2FdoBasic-Search%3FQuery%3Dcalderwood%26amp%3Bfilter%3Di-id%253A10.2307%252Fi239751&seq=18#page_scan_tab_contents, 41; American Prohibition Yearbook 1915, 94; "Remember When, 1910", Compiled by Don McNeil, Shakopee Heritage Society, From the Shakopee-Argus Tribune, ShakopeeHeritage. org, October 3rd, 2015, Accessed July 4, 2016, http://www.sha-kopeeheritage.org/historic-articles/remember-when/remem-ber-when-1910/;

6. Who's Who In Illinois, 1045; Who's who in America, Volume 9,376

7. American Advance, 7; 23; 33; 85; "No Steam Roller For Prohibitionists", New York Times, (New York, NY), July 12, 1912, Reproduced Online in, A WWI Diary That Never Was, July 12, 2012, Accessed July 29, 2016, http://wwidiary.blogspot. com/2012/07/no-steam-roller-for-prohibitionists.html

8. Who's who in America, Volume 9,376

9. "Our Campaigns - Candidate - Willis Greenleaf Calderwood." Our Campaigns, Accessed April 10, 2017, http://www.ourcam-paigns.com/CandidateDetail.html?CandidateID=36038

10. Caine to Caldom", Index to Politicians, Political Graveyard. com, Accessed July 5, 2016, http://politicalgraveyard.com/bio/caine-caldom.html; "Our Campaigns - Candidate - Willis Greenleaf Calderwood."; American Prohibition Yearbook 1916, Ed. John A. Shields, (Chicago: Prohibition National Committee, 1916), https://books.google.com/books?hl=en&lr=&id=lUX-iAAAAMAAJ&oi=fnd&pg=PA2&dq=w.g.+calderwood&ots=x-BrYYavDBM&sig=zCtEk7lQ5mYqtvHvFZ3R3efrVV4#v=onep-

age&q=w.g.%20calderwood&f=false, 138-139

11. American Prohibition Yearbook 1915, 19; Who's Who In Illinois, 1045; Lisa M. Anderson, The Politics of Prohibition: American Governance and the Prohibition Party, (New York: Cambridge University Press, 2013), 240-241

12. Anderson, The Politics of Prohibition, 191-281; The National Advocate Issue 4, (National Temperance Society, 1917), https://books. google.com/books?id=8CAzAQAAMAAJ&pg=RA1-PA115&lp-g=RA1-PA115&dq=a+maker+of+men+by+w.g.+calderwood&-source=bl&ots=ZD0_j7mPVZ&sig=xSp_out3mcNTjJ7c-BoQLdB1oMM4&hl=en&sa=X&ei=tJGVVfaFNIPo-QG-c4bS4Dg&ved=0CCQQ6AEwAw#v=onepage&q=%20w.g.%20 calderwood&f=false, 85-137; Thomas R. Pegram, "Prohibition", In The American Congress: The Building of Democracy, edited by Julian E. Zelizer, (Boston: Houghton Mifflin, 2004), Academic OneFile (accessed April 10, 2017), http://go.galegroup.com/ ps/i.do?p=AONE&sw=w&u=suny_ceramics&v=2.1&it=r&id=-GALE%7CA176869503&sid=summon&asid=7cb0b52f0c-1f2299155a81d90cefd6ac

13. The National Advocate Issue 4, 85-37

14. Roger Storms, Partisan Prophets, (Denver: National Prohibition Foundation Inc., 1972), https://archive.org/details/Parti-sanProphetsAHistoryOfTheProhibitionParty1854-1972, 27-48; Pegram, "Prohibition"

15. "FOR BRYAN AND SUNDAY.; W.G. Calder-Wood Thinks They Should Head Prohibition Ticket", New York Times. (New York City, New York). July 17, 1920 http://query.nytimes.com/gst/ abstract.html?res=9402EFDD1131E433A25754C1A9619C-946195D6CF&url=http://timesmachine.nytimes.com/times-machine/1920/07/17/102872878.html; "DRYS IN STAMPEDE NOMINATE BRYAN: Vote Him, Willing or Not, Their Party Standard Bearer in Coming Campaign.--WOMAN CHAIRMAN LEADS--Delegates, Impatient at Talk of Refusal, Parade and Shout for Convention Nominee. Bryan's Word to " Dry " Champions. DRYS IN STAMPEDE NOMINATE BRYAN Wanted Bry-

an, Willing or Not. Some for Billy Sunday or Henry Ford", New York Times, (New York, N.Y), 22 July 1920: 1., http://ezproxy. alfred.edu:2053/docview/98178642/F9E95FA8C1FA4E3F-PQ/18?accountid=8263

16. Britannica Academic, s.v. "William Jennings Bryan," accessed April 10, 2017, http://ezproxy.alfred.edu:2838/levels/colle-giate/article/William-Jennings-Bryan/16819

17. Britannica Academic, s.v. "Billy Sunday," accessed April 10, 2017, http://ezproxy.alfred.edu:2838/levels/collegiate/article/ Billy-Sunday/70353

18. "DRY FORCE WINNING AUSTRALIAN FIGHT: Workers Face Big Difficulty in Reaching Dwellers of the "Back-Country" Made Record Campaign Wide Education Required Difficult but Inter-esting", The Christian Science Monitor, (Boston, Mass), 12 July 1922: 3.; Who's Who In Illinois, 1045

19. Who's Who In Illinois, 1045

20. "Drys Open Barrage of Facts To Discount Wet Propaganda: Expose Claims of Millions Employed in Beer Trade and Show Farmer Little Benefited--Prove Other Assertions Wrong Dry Facts Presented Against Wet Report Dry Facts for Press Vir-ginia Presbyterians Own Guides on Dry Law Montclair, New Jersey, Tightens Drink Law North Carolina Voters Urged to Support Drys McBride Says Primaries Have Dashed Wet Hopes New York Third Party Candidates Expected", Special to The Christian Science Monitor, The Christian Science Monitor (Bos-ton, Mass), 26 Sep 1932: 1., http://ezproxy.alfred.edu:2053/ docview/513250058/FFCE3ACFEF5244A7PQ/22?accoun-tid=8263

21. "Willis G. Calderwood", Como History, Accessed April 10, 2017, https://sites.google.com/a/comogreenvillage.info/como-histo-ry/home/people-of-the-past-documents/willis-calderwood

22. W.G. Calderwood, A. Lincoln: Reformer: Born February 9, 1809, (Minneapolis: Cole and Christianson Co. Publishers, 1909), https://archive.org/details/alincolnreformer3483cald;

"Talks on Temperance", Duluth Evening Herald, (Duluth, Minnesota), July 15, 1909, https://www.myheritage.com/research/collection-90100/compilation-of-published-sources?itemId=453275004&action=showRecord

23. W.G. Calderwood, "Prohibition as a Present Political Platform", The Annals of the American Academy of Political and Social Science 32 (1908): 106-11, http://www.jstor.org/stable/1010558, 108

24. Calderwood, "Prohibition as a Present Political Platform", 106-111

25. W.G. Calderwood, "Fargo and Morehead – A Contrast; Prohibition and High License Side By Side", The Reform Bulletin: A Weekly Report from the New York Volumes 1-4, (Albany, New York: O.R. Miller, 1910), https://books.google.com/books?id=INwpAAAAYAAJ&pg=PT136&lpg=PT136&dq=w.g.+calderwood+1889&source=bl&ots=R5u7TINjde&sig=NVOCE8nbrA-Jablm5VibTQkw71I&hl=en&sa=X-&ved=0ahUKEwjEutrcqM7NAhXL2SYKHTEGCy8Q6AEIK-TAD#v=onepage&q=w.g.%20calderwood%201889&f=false; American Prohibition Yearbook 1915, 113-114; 126-127

26. W.G. Calderwood, "Wet-Dry Hearings Brought Out That Illicit Liquor Made in This Country Equaled Three Gallons a Day for Each Individual, or Twice as Much as pre-Volstead Consumption a Year, Letter to The Post Says, Calling It "An Exaggerated Case of Exaggera- tion", Minneapolis, Minn., Aug. 19. The Washington Post, (Washington, D.C) 22 Aug 1926: S2,http://ezproxy.alfred.edu:2053/docview/149671900?pq-origsite=summon&accountid=8263

27. W.G. Calderwood, "All Unfulfilled Promise", New York Times, (New York, N.Y), 31 July 1934: 16, http://ezproxy.alfred.edu:2053/docview/101056464?pq-origsite=summon&accountid=8263; W.G. Calderwood, "Big Shrinkage in Estimates of Beer Revenue Since the Campaign", Minneapolis, Minn., The Washington Post (Washington, D.C), 23 Mar 1933: 6, http://ezproxy.alfred.edu:2053/docview/150408730?pq-origsite=-

summon&accountid=8263

28. W.G. Calderwood, "Why Not Relax Murder Laws", New York Times, (New York, N.Y), 11 July 1926: X8, http://ezproxy.alfred.edu:2053/docview/103775877?pq-origsite=summon&accountid=8263

29. W.G. Calderwood, Prohibition Facts: Questions and Answers, (Minneapolis: Prohibition Facts Service, 1932), https://babel.hathitrust.org/cgi/pt?id=mdp.39015071421302;view=1up;seq=1; W.G. Calderwood, Prohibition Facts: Questions and Answers, (Minneapolis: Prohibition Facts Service, 1933), https://babel.hathitrust.org/cgi/pt?id=mdp.39015071420809; W.G. Calderwood, Prohibition Facts: Questions and Answers, (Minneapolis: Prohibition Facts Service, 1935), https://babel.hathitrust.org/cgi/pt?id=mdp.39015071420783;view=1up;seq=3

30. Calderwood, Prohibition Facts, 1933

31. Calderwood, Prohibition Facts, 1935

32. W.G. Calderwood, Temperance Facts, (Minneapolis: Minnesota Temperance Movement, 1940), https://babel.hathitrust.org/cgi/pt?id=mdp.39015071420817;view=1up;seq=2

33. Alice Felt Tyler, Freedom's Ferment – Phases of American Social History to 1860, (Minneapolis: University of Minnesota Press, 1944), 308-350

34. Tyler, Freedom's Ferment, 308-350; Calderwood, Temperance Facts, 84-88

35. Tyler, Freedom's Ferment, 308-350; Calderwood, Temperance Facts, 84-88; Pegram, "Prohibition"

36. Henry S. Clubb, The Maine liquor law; its origin, history, and results, including a life of Hon. Neal Dow, (New York: Pub. for the Maine Law Statistical Society, by Fowler and Wells, 1856), https://babel.hathitrust.org/cgi/pt?id=uc2.ark:/13960/t3fx-76t0v, 7-68; 99-296

37. Clubb, The Maine liquor law, 269-429

38. Storms, Partisan Prophets, 1-23; "1872 Prohibition Party Plat-

form", Prohibitionists.org, Accessed April 10, 2017, http://www.prohibitionists.org/background/party_platform/Platform1872.htm

39. Storms, Partisan Prophets, 1-23; "1872 Prohibition Party Platform"; Anderson, The Politics of Prohibition, 1-98

40. Pegram, "Prohibition"; Anderson, The Politics of Prohibition, 99-281

41. Anderson, The Politics of Prohibition, 191-281; The National Advocate Issue 4, 85-137; Storms, Partisan Prophets, 27-48

42. Anderson, The Politics of Prohibition, 279; Storms, Partisan Prophets, 37-50

43. Calderwood, Temperance Facts, 48-56

44. "Gene Amondson's Life, Art and Mission", GeneAmondson.com, Accessed April 09, 2017, http://www.geneamondson.com/

45. Peter B. Gemma, "Interview with James Hedges, Prohibition Party nominee for President", Independent Political Report, August 22, 2016. Accessed April 09, 2017, http://independentpoliticalreport.com/2016/08/interview-with-james-hedges-prohibition-party-nominee-for-president/; Billy Joe Parker to Ben Baker. Letters in "In search of rational thinking." Pork Brains with Milk Gravy. January 03, 2017. Accessed April 09, 2017. http://porkbrainsandmilkgravy.blogspot.com/2017/01/in-search-of-rational-thinking.html

46. Billy Joe Parker to Ben Baker, Letters; Billy Joe Parker. e-mail message to the members of the Prohibition Party email list. August 23, 2016.

Bibliography

"1872 Prohibition Party Platform." Prohibitionists.org. Accessed April 10, 2017. http://www.prohibitionists.org/background/ party_platform/Platform1872.htm

Abbott, Kathryn A. "Alcohol and the Anishinaabeg of Minnesota in the Early Twentieth Century". *The Western Historical Quarterly* 30. no. 1 (1999): 25-43. http://ezproxy.alfred. edu:2122/stable/971157?Search=yes&resultItemClick=true&-searchText=calderwood&searchUri=%2Faction%2FdoBasic-Search%3FQuery%3Dcalderwood%26amp%3Bfilter%3Di-id%253A10.2307%252Fi239751&seq=18#page_scan_tab_contents

Abbott, Kathryn A. "Liquor law in Minnesota Indian country in the early twentieth century". *Legal Studies Forum* 25, no. 3/4 (January 2, 2001): 567-585. *OmniFile Full Text Select (H.W. Wilson).* EBSCO*host* (accessed July 3, 2016)

American Advance. Chicago: Prohibition National Committee, 1911. https://books.google.com/books?id=XTniAAAAMAAJ&-source=gbs_navlinks_s

American Prohibition Yearbook 1915. Ed. John A. Shields. Chicago: Prohibition National Committee, 1915. https://books. google.com/books?id=22RDAQAAMAAJ&pg=PA20&lp-g=PA20&dq=a+maker+of+men+by+w.g.+calderwood&-source=bl&ots=sBX6rfev6Y&sig=a8p-FFYvWY2_RF7f-BRZV2jiHY_E&hl=en&sa=X&ei=tJGVVfaFNIPo-QG-c4bS4Dg&ved=0CC4Q6AEwBg#v=onepage&q=%20w.g.%20 calderwood&f=false

American Prohibition Yearbook 1916. Ed. John A. Shields. Chicago: Prohibition National Committee, 1916. https:// books.google.com/books?hl=en&lr=&id=lUXiAAAAMAA-J&oi=fnd&pg=PA2&dq=w.g.+calderwood&ots=xBrYYa-vDBM&sig=zCtEk7lQ5mYqtvHvFZ3R3efrVV4#v=onep-age&q=w.g.%20calderwood&f=false

Andersen, Lisa. "From Unpopular to Excluded: Prohibitionists and the Ascendancy of a Democratic-Republican System, 1888–1912". *Journal of Policy History* 24, no. 2 (2012): 288-318. https://muse.jhu.edu/ (accessed June 30, 2016)

Anderson, Lisa M. *The Politics of Prohibition: American Governance and the Prohibition Party.* New York: Cambridge University Press, 2013.

Billy Joe Parker. e-mail message to the members of the Prohibition Party email list. August 23, 2016.

Billy Joe Parker to Ben Baker. In "In search of rational thinking." Pork Brains with Milk Gravy. January 03, 2017. Accessed April 09, 2017. http://porkbrainsandmilkgravy.blogspot. com/2017/01/in-search-of-rational-thinking.html

Britannica Academic, s.v. "Billy Sunday". accessed April 10, 2017. http://ezproxy.alfred.edu:2838/levels/collegiate/article/Billy-Sunday/70353.

Britannica Academic, s.v. "William Jennings Bryan". accessed April 10, 2017. http://ezproxy.alfred.edu:2838/levels/collegiate/article/William-Jennings-Bryan/16819.

"Caine to Caldom", Index to Politicians, Political Graveyard.com, Accessed July 5, 2016, http://politicalgraveyard.com/bio/caine-caldom.html

Calderwood, W.G. *A. Lincoln: Reformer: Born February 9, 1809.* Minneapolis: Cole and Christianson Co. Publishers, 1909. https://archive.org/details/alincolnreformer3483cald

Calderwood, W.G. "All Unfulfilled Promise". *New York Times* (New York, N.Y) 31 July 1934: 16. http://ezproxy.alfred.edu:2053/docview/101056464?pq-origsite=summon&accountid=8263

Calderwood, W.G. "Big Shrinkage in Estimates of Beer Revenue Since the Campaign". Minneapolis, Minn.. The Washington Post (Washington, D.C) 23 Mar 1933: 6. http://ezproxy.alfred.edu:2053/docview/150408730?pq-origsite=summon&accountid=8263

Calderwood, W.G. "Fargo and Morehead – A Contrast; *Prohibition and High License Side By Side". The Reform Bulletin: A Weekly Report from the New York Volumes 1-4.* Albany, New York: O.R. Miller, 1910. https://books.google.com/books?id=INwpAAAAYAAJ&pg=PT136&lpg=PT136&dq=w.g.+calderwood+1889&source=bl&ots=R5u7TINjde&sig=NVOCE8nbrA-Jablm5VibTQkw71I&hl=en&sa=X-&ved=0ahUKEwjEutrcqM7NAhXL2SYKHTEGCy8Q6AEIKTAD#v=onepage&q=w.g.%20calderwood%201889&f=false

Calderwood, W.G. "Prohibition as a Present Political Platform", *The Annals of the American Academy of Political and Social Science* 32 (1908): 106-11, http://www.jstor.org/stable/1010558

Calderwood, W.G. *Prohibition Facts: Questions and Answers.* Minneapolis: Prohibition Facts Service, 1932. https://babel.hathitrust.org/cgi/pt?id=mdp.39015071421302;view=1up;seq=1

Calderwood, W.G. *Prohibition Facts: Questions and Answers.* Minneapolis: Prohibition Facts Service, 1933. https://babel.hathitrust.org/cgi/pt?id=mdp.39015071420809

Calderwood, W.G. *Prohibition Facts: Questions and Answers.* Minneapolis: Prohibition Facts Service, 1935. https://babel.hathitrust.org/cgi/pt?id=mdp.39015071420783;view=1up;seq=3

Calderwood, W.G. Temperance Facts. Minneapolis: Minnesota Temperance Movement, 1940. https://babel.hathitrust.org/cgi/pt?id=mdp.39015071420817;view=1up;seq=2

Calderwood, W.G. "Wet-Dry Hearings Brought Out That Illicit Liquor Made in This Country Equaled Three Gallons a Day for Each Individual, or Twice as Much as pre-Volstead Consumption a Year, Letter to The Post Says, Calling It "An Exaggerated Case of Exaggera- tion." Minneapolis, Minn., Aug. 19. The Washington Post. (Washington, D.C) 22 Aug 1926: S2.http://ezproxy.alfred.edu:2053/docview/149671900?pq-origsite=summon&accountid=8263

Calderwood, W.G. "Why Not Relax Murder Laws". New York Times. (New York, N.Y) 11 July 1926: X8. http://ezproxy.alfred.edu:2053/docview/103775877?pq-origsite=summon&accountid=8263

City of Minneapolis. *Annual Reports of the Various City Officers of the City of Minneapolis Minnesota For The Year 1909.* Minneapolis: Syndicate Printing Company, 1910. https://books.google.com/books?id=6KEaAQAAMAAJ&pg=RA1-PR68&lpg=RA1-PR68&dq=w.g.+calderwood&source=bl&ots=IehLoEMJ3K&sig=Gw5hVdwF2FMYo3mApvuko2KWZb-M&hl=en&sa=X&ei=ER-UVZjLGMnksAWzxYj4BQ&ved=0CEUQ6AEwCA#v=snippet&q=brewing&f=false

Clubb, Henry S. The Maine liquor law; its origin, history, and results, including a life of Hon. Neal Dow. New York: Pub. for the Maine Law Statistical Society, by Fowler and Wells, 1856. https://babel.hathitrust.org/cgi/pt?id=uc2.ark:/13960/t3fx-76tov

"DRY FORCE WINNING AUSTRALIAN FIGHT: Workers Face Big Difficulty in Reaching Dwellers of the "Back-Country" Made Record Campaign Wide Education Required Difficult but Interesting". The *Christian Science Monitor*. (Boston, Mass). 12 July 1922: 3.

"DRYS IN STAMPEDE NOMINATE BRYAN: Vote Him, Willing or Not, Their Party Standard Bearer in Coming Campaign.--WOMAN CHAIRMAN LEADS--Delegates, Impatient at Talk of Refusal, Parade and Shout for Convention Nominee. Bryan's Word to " Dry " Champions. DRYS IN STAMPEDE NOMINATE BRYAN Wanted Bryan, Willing or Not. Some for Billy Sunday or Henry Ford". *New York Times*. (New York, N.Y). 22 July 1920: 1. http://ezproxy.alfred.edu:2053/docview/98178642/F9E95FA8C1FA4E3FPQ/18?accountid=8263

"Drys Open Barrage of Facts To Discount Wet Propaganda: Expose Claims of Millions Employed in Beer Trade and Show Farmer Little Benefited--Prove Other Assertions Wrong Dry Facts Presented Against Wet Report Dry Facts for Press Virginia Presbyterians Own Guides on Dry Law Montclair, New Jersey, Tightens Drink Law North Carolina Voters Urged to Support Drys McBride Says Primaries Have Dashed Wet Hopes New York Third Party Candidates Expected". Special to The Christian Science Monitor. *The Christian Science Monitor* (Boston, Mass). 26 Sep 1932: 1. http://ezproxy.alfred.edu:2053/docview/513250058/FFCE3ACFEF5244A7PQ/22?accountid=8263

"FOR BRYAN AND SUNDAY.; W.G. Calder-Wood Thinks They Should Head Prohibition Ticket". *New York Times*. (New York City, New York). July 17, 1920. http://query.nytimes.com/gst/abstract.html?res=9402EFDD1131E433A25754C1A9619C-946195D6CF&url=http://timesmachine.nytimes.com/timesmachine/1920/07/17/102872878.html

Gemma, Peter B. "Interview with James Hedges, Prohibition Party nominee for President." Independent Political Report. August 22, 2016. Accessed April 09, 2017. http://independentpoliticalreport.com/2016/08/interview-with-james-hedges-prohibition-party-nominee-for-president/

"Gene Amondson's Life, Art and Mission." GeneAmondson.com. Accessed April 09, 2017. http://www.geneamondson.com/.

Hammell, George M. *The Passing of the Saloon: An Authentic and Official Presentation of the Anti-Liquor Crusade in America*. Cincinnati: The Tower Press, 1908. https://books.google.com/books?hl=en&lr=&id=q1zlAAAAMAAJ&oi=fnd&pg=PR11&dq=w.g.+calderwood&ots=vwHIuTnz2G&sig=kEzBPcgSTWl-rdlFIW_-OxOI5H8A#v=onepage&q=w.g.%20calderwood&f=false

Hill, John Wesley. *Twin City Methodism: Being a History of the Methodist Episcopal Church in Minneapolis and St. Paul Minn.*. Ed. Minneapolis: Price Bros. Publishing Co., 1895. https://books.google.com/books?id=QoUVAAAAYAA-J&pg=PA116&lpg=PA116&dq=willis+g+calderwood+die&-source=bl&ots=7VT2WmlaOF&sig=TqHuphbC1xv9SS0CT_cixwuOUI4&hl=en&ei=MpdXTazvGIGC8gbbvozQBw&sa=X-&oi=book_result&ct=result&resnum=2&ved=0CBwQ6A-EwAQ#v=onepage&q=calderwood&f=false

Hudson, Horace B. *A Half Century of Minneapolis*. Minneapolis: The Hudson Publishing Company, 1908. https://books.google.com/books?id=F2ZAAAAAYAAJ&pg=PA493&lpg=PA493&dq=willis+greenleaf+calderwood&-source=bl&ots=NrjNiMG-pA&sig=LVMdNmTxwgYuyS209Gb-2DoTZ-sk&hl=en&sa=X&ei=pMCXVbaaEIT_-AHGoo-rACA&ved=0CD4Q6AEwBzgK#v=onepage&q=willis%20greenleaf%20calderwood&f=false

"No Steam Roller For Prohibitionists". *New York Times*. (New York, NY). July 12, 1912. Reproduced Online in, *A WWI Diary That Never Was*. July 12, 2012. Accessed July 29, 2016. http://wwidiary.blogspot.com/2012/07/no-steam-roller-for-prohibitionists.html

Pegram, Thomas R. "Prohibition." In *The American Congress*: *The Building of Democracy*, edited by Julian E. Zelizer. Boston: Houghton Mifflin, 2004. *Academic OneFile* (accessed April 10, 2017). http://go.galegroup.com/ps/i.do?p=AONE&sw=w&u=suny_ceramics&v=2.1&it=r&id=-GALE%7CA176869503&sid=summon&asid=7cb0b52f0c-1f2299155a81d90cefd6ac

"Remember When, 1910". Compiled by Don McNeil, Shakopee Heritage Society. From the Shakopee-Argus Tribune. ShakopeeHeritage.org. October 3rd, 2015, Accessed July 4, 2016. http://www.shakopeeheritage.org/historic-articles/remember-when/remember-when-1910/

Storms, Roger. *Partisan Prophets*. Denver: National Prohibition Foundation Inc., 1972. https://archive.org/details/Partisan-ProphetsAHistoryOfTheProhibitionParty1854-1972

"Talks on Temperance". Duluth Evening Herald. (Duluth, Minnesota). July 15, 1909. https://www.myheritage.com/research/collection-90100/compilation-of-published-sources?itemId=453275004&action=showRecord

The National Advocate Issue 4. National Temperance Society, 1917. https://books.google.com/books?id=8CAzAQAAMAAJ&pg=RA1-PA115&lpg=RA1-PA115&dq=a+maker+of+men+by+w.g.+calderwood&source=bl&ots=ZD0_j7mPVZ&sig=xSp_out3mcNTjJ7c-BoQLdB1oMM4&hl=en&sa=X&ei=tJGVVfaFNIP0-QGc4bS4Dg&ved=0CCQQ6AEwAw#v=onepage&q=%20w.g.%20calderwood&f=false

Tyler, Alice Felt. *Freedom's Ferment – Phases of American Social History to 1860.* Minneapolis: University of Minnesota Press, 1944.

Who's who in America, Volume 9. Ed. John William Leonard and Albert Nelson Marquis. Chicago: A. N. Marquis and Company, 1916. https://books.google.com/books?id=OlIlod0IyTkC&pg=PA376&lpg=PA376&dq=willis+greenleaf+calderwood&source=bl&ots=jUHNnd-NR1&sig=RpTXEinG-qR2AfM-riyZ16IajxTY&hl=en&sa=X&ei=X9CXVYOlEYWu-QGfzb6ABA&ved=0CCwQ6AEwADgU#v=onepage&q=willis%20greenleaf%20calderwood&f=false

"Willis G. Calderwood." *Como History.* Accessed April 10, 2017. https://sites.google.com/a/comogreenvillage.info/como-history/home/people-of-the-past-documents/willis-calderwood

Note on the text

This edition is based on the original 1940 edition, accessed through a digitized version on Babel Hathitrust. The edition of this book has aimed to keep the text as close to the original text as plausible. The font style, spelling, grammar, and punctuation of the text has been produced as it appeared in the original version. The tables were recreated using modern software and aim to be as close to the original as possible. The graphs within the text are from a digitized version of the book, in Babel Hathitrust.

Calderwood Timeline

Historical Context

1869: Prohibition Party Formed

1917; U.S. Enters World War II, U.S. Senate Proposes Prohibition Amendment

1918; Temporary Wartime Prohibition Act Passed

1919; 18th Amendment passed

1929; Beginning of Great Depression

1933; Passage of 21st Amendment, ending national prohibition

Life

1866, July 25; W.G. Calderwood born in Fox Lake, Dodge County Wisconsin, to John Calderwood and Emily Bethiah (Greenleaf) Calderwood

1882 enters the Wasoja Seminary

1886; Graduates from Wesleyan Methodist Seminary of Wasioja, MN

1889; starts work at the Commercial College in Minneapolis Works, From 1889-1903 Began his activities in the Prohibition Party

1890; Graduates from Am. Corr. U. in Chicago

1892; begins affiliation with Methodist Episcopal Church in Minneapolis

June 9, 1892; Marries Alice M. Cox

1897; Becomes Executive Secretary of the of Minnesota Prohibition State Committee Serves in this position from 1897-1910

1900; Becomes organizer and treasurer for Ministers Life and Casualty Union, did from 1900-1938

1902; Calderwood goes to the state committee with a report on public sentiment, making the case that it was time to start seeking out to win political offices. Minnesota Prohibitionists electoral successes in an election after the pass of election law helped national party realize that they could benefit by concentration campaigns.

1903; Ends work at the Commercial College. Starts work at the Northwestern Life Insurance Company. Works From 1903-1907. Attends May Northwestern Prohibition Conference in Sioux City Iowa, as president of his district.

1905; Becomes Secretary of National Prohibition Committee. Holds Position From 1905-1912.

1906; Calderwood Heads the campaign effort to expand prohibition party support and get people elected to office in Minnesota. Succeeded in raising vote levels by large amounts in each election cycle. Minnesota State Prohibition Party Sues the State of Minnesota over ballot access and the court decided that the party was entitled ballot access.

1907; Ended work at the Northwestern Insurance Company.

1909; Calderwood is involved in several lawsuits against brewers and the city of Minneapolis in order to make them return the refunds that Minneapolis had given for canceling their liquor licenses.

Calderwood publishes A. Lincoln: Reformer: Born February 12, 1809.

1910; End of position as executive secretary of state committee. Becomes Chairman of the state committee.

Held position from 1910-1914. Due to the research of figures like Calderwood, treaties with the Chippewa Indians against alcohol were enforced.

1911; there's speculation that Calderwood may get the party chairmanship or 1912 presidential nomination. March 1st in the annual banquet the State Prohibition Party rejects Optionists and moves for advocating for a state constitutional amendment for prohibition. Calderwood was part of the decision severing from the optionists.

1912; End of position as National Secretary. Becomes member of National Prohibition Executive Committee. Runs for Congress. At the Prohibition national convention he was one of the people considered for new party chairman. A compromise candidate was chosen, and Calderwood was one of the extremes passed over, due to being favored by the insurgent element.

1913; July 09, 1913, On a streetcar, a man steel's W.G. Calderwood's handbag, mistaking it for a jewel case; when it only has prohibitionist literature. Calderwood says he hopes he reads it and does him some good. He then goes to a conference to speak on how to spread prohibitionist literature.

1914; End of position as Chairman of the state committee. Ran for Governor. On Prohibition executive committee, on national committee, and chairman of state committee. December 30th, Calderwood delivers speech as part of the December 29th to January 1st 1915 national conference of the Intercollegiate Prohibition Association, on party platforms.

He is the campaign director for Charles Randell's congressional campaign. Randell becomes the first Prohibition Party candidate to win election into congress.

1915; Calderwood is Executive Secretary of the Prohibition Party North Central Division. 260 Dry Towns, 6 completely dry counties, 54 Towns voted dry in Minnesota. April 27th, Calderwood gives lecture at Harvard on the making of a political campaign. Directed the campaign of prohibition candidate William Shaw for governor of Massachusetts.

1916; Ran for Senate on Prohibition ticket. Was an organizer for the Minister's Casualty Union. He is the Minnesota Representative for the National Convention. His 1916 Senate Race receives 78,425 votes; 20.58% of the vote. Calderwood did better than the democratic candidate in 26 districts. Calderwood was also considered as a possible candidate in the convention for selecting a presidential candidate in 1916. He received 22 votes and 2.98% of the vote; coming in fourth place. Calderwood was a candidate for delegate at large in Prohibition Presidential Preference Primary ballot for candidate Eugene Floss. Calderwood is vice chairman for the national committee, and is on the national executive committee of the prohibition party.

1917; By July Calderwood has called for national wartime prohibition. He is the executive secretary of the committee of sixty on wartime prohibition.

1918; Runs for Senate on the Nationalist Party ticket. April 30, 1918, Calderwood temporarily left the Prohibition Party to run for Senate in Minnesota on the Ticket of the National Party (a short lived political coalition of Pro-war socialists, Prohibitionists, Suffragists, Progressives, and the like). Endorsed by Democrat St. Paul Mayor Lawrence c. Hodgson.

1919; Calderwood is the vice-chairman of the national executive committee for the prohibition party and the national committee member for Minnesota.

1920; April 20th, 1920, Calderwood succeeds in preventing railroad shipments of liquor to 37 towns under the territory of the Indian treaty of 1863.

July 17, 1920, Calderwood supported having William Jennings Bryan and Billy Sunday. He attempts at the convention to have Bryan nominated. Bryan turns down offer and the motion to nominate him fails.

1921, by this time Calderwood is fact checking efforts in favor of Prohibition. Starts campaigning for prohibition in Australia. Runs campaign in Australia from 1921-1923.

1923, finishes campaign in Australia [P2, 26]. It is indicated that he may have went on a tour of Philippines, Japan, China, and India after the Australian Election.

1927; February 11 1927, Calderwood receives letter from Ida Tarbell responding to his inquiries about Lincoln's stance on prohibition.

1932; Calderwood is the head of the Prohibition Facts service, a group dedicated to factually countering wet propaganda.

Calderwood begins publishing his Prohibition Facts series, with first *Prohibition Facts*.

1933: the second *Prohibition Facts* is published.

1935: the third *Prohibition Facts* is published

1938; Becomes director of the civic and organizational departments of the Minnesota Temperance Movement, and does so until 1942.

1939; goes on another prohibition campaign in Australia, lasting into 1940.

1940; finishes second Australia Campaign.

Calderwood publishes *Temperance Facts*.

1942; finishes as director of the civic and organizational departments of the Minnesota Temperance Movement.

1956, W.G. Calderwood dies

TEMPERANCE FACTS

The purpose of this booklet is to provide students and others with authenticated facts bearing on the liquor problem, and the most successful efforts of society to combat the social and economic evils that grow out of the traffic in intoxicants.

It is a book of facts, with references to the sources, which affords a guide for the student who wishes to pursue the study further to sources of information. The topical arrangement makes the book desirable for teachers and students in schools, and young people's groups.

Its small compass makes it convenient for the pocket or hand bag, yet it contains more material than many books of double the size and much greater cost.

It is ideal for writers, editors, pastors, teachers, and speakers —for public and church schools and colleges— for reading rooms and libraries—for study text—for general sale and distribution.

FOREWARD

This booklet is Number Four in a series in which the records of the political, economic, social and moral havoc of the traffic in intoxicating beverages have been presented.

This number has a distinct advantage over its predecessors, since it is now possible to contrast the record of repeal, with its devastating evils, with the benefits of prohibition. That drunkenness is bad for the individual is agreed to by the fanatical drinker as well as by the fanatical abstainer. And it seems axiomatic that that which is bad for a person is also bad for a people.

This issue, in common with the earlier numbers, is an honest effort to examine the facts rather than a discussion of the policies or principles involved. Therefore the compiler says little and quotes much. The quotations are generously documented, not only for the purpose of validation, but also to enable the student to examine the subject further by consulting the works from which the statements or figures are extracted.

Moreover there is a sustained avoidance of argumentation. Authenticated facts are persuasive. Social facts are the verified records of human history, the proven conclusions of human experience.

The Noble Experiment

Q. Did National Prohibition substantially reduce drinking and its evil consequences?

A. If it did, every patriot and every lover of life, liberty and the pursuit of happiness should be for it. If it did not, every true American should oppose it. That question goes straight to the heart of the whole problem. All that follows, has but one purpose—a clear understanding of, and a true answer to that fundamental question.

Q. What did the Revolutionary Fathers think?

A. In 1678, which was 98 years before the signing of the Declaration of Independence, our patriot forefathers in New Jersey prohibited the sale of liquor to Indians; and in 1733, Georgia prohibited the importation of liquor into that colony.

The first Continental Congress, only 7 months and 23 days after the signing of the Declaration of Independence, resolved:

That it be recommended to the several Legislatures of the United States immediately to pass laws the most effectual for putting an immediate stop to the pernicious practice of distilling grain, by which the most extensive evils are likely to be derived, if not quickly prevented. (PTJ—p. 13)

Our early presidents seemed to be a braver breed than those of the 20th century; for George Washington, the Father of his country, in a letter dated March 31, 1789, only a few days before he was inducted into the office of Chief Magistrate of the nation, denounced drink as "the source of all evil and the ruin of half the working men in the country." (PU p. 14)

John Adams, the second President, condemned the traffic most severely, denouncing it as an arch corrupter of politics. On February 29, 1760, he wrote in his diary:

"But the worst effect of all, and which ought to make every man who has the least sense of his privileges tremble, these houses are become the nurseries of our legislators. An artful man, who has neither sense nor sentiment, may, by gaining a little sway among the rabble of a town, multiply taverns and dramshops and thereby secure the votes of taverner and retailer and of all: and the multiplication of taverns will make many, who may be induced by flip and rum, to vote for any man whatever." (PU p. 14).

After eight years as President, Thomas Jefferson, author of the Declaration of Independence and the third President, is reported to have said:

"The habit of using ardent spirits by men in public office has produced more injury to the public service, and more trouble to me, than any other circumstance that has occurred in the internal concerns of the country during my administration." (PU p. 14).

From those early Colonial days until now, the greatest political, social and moral incubus of the nation has been the beverage liquor traffic.

Abraham Lincoln, called the Saviour of His Country, speaking on Washington's birthday, in 1842, said:

"Whether or not the world would be vastly benefitted by a total and final banishment from it of all intoxicating drinks seems to me not now an open question. Three-fourths of mankind confess the affirmative with their tongues and, I believe, all the rest acknowledge it in their hearts ....

"If the relative grandeur of revolutions shall be estimated by the great amount of human misery they alleviate, and the small amount they inflict, then indeed will this be the grandest the world shall ever have seen." (AL pp. 82, 84).

The Founders and the Saviour of our Nation saw in the liquor traffic a danger, indeed THE danger, to the perpetuity of the republic.

Q. Were people drinking more or less in Colonial days?

A. Doubtless much less, though we have no official record of the amount of liquor consumed until 1840. However, when Lincoln delivered his Washingtonian address, from which the above quotation is taken, the annual consumption of intoxicants totalled 4.17 gallons per capita; and in 1911 it reached an all-time high of 22.81 gallons for every man, woman and baby. This was an increase of 447% in the per capita consumption of intoxicants. In other words the consumption of intoxicants in the United States had increased 4.47 times faster than the population.

   4.17 gallons per capita, 1840

22.81 gallons per capita, 1911

Q. Weren't the people doing anything to check this alarming situation?

A. Yes. Some preachers began to preach against drink and for total abstinence long before the birth of the nation. In 1808 when the Republic was 32 years old, the first voluntary total abstinence society in the world, of which an authentic record has been preserved, was organized in Saratoga County, New York. It was named "The Union Temperate Society of Moreau and Northumberland." It was later known as "The Billy Clark Temperance Society." (SE Vol. 2, pp 620-4). Thereafter many other organizations, including the Sons of Temperance, the Independent Order of Good Templars, which at one time had a membership of a quarter million, the "Blue Ribbon" movement, the spectacular "Father Matthew Movement," and the Woman's Christian Temperance Union, which is the largest world temperance organization in the history of the race, and is still growing fast, and going strong. Its membership in America is a quarter of a million. The Prohibition Party pledged to the prohibition of manufacture, sale, transportation, importation, and exportation of intoxicating; liquor for beverage purposes was organized in the city of Chicago in 1869, and has bad a national and many state tickets in the field every general election since.

Q. Did this great educational drive sharply reduce per capita drinking?

A. Probably no student of the times would doubt that these agencies did check the rate of increase in drinking. But, in spite of all these "moral suasion" movements, the per capita drinking continued to climb. In other words, in the face of all this educational work the liquor interests, with their huge profits and aggressive merchandising, were able to more than match the influence of the churches and temperance organizations and steadily to increase the per capita consumption of intoxicants with all of the attendant physical, social, moral and political evils. The per person use of intoxicants climbed by 447 per cent in 60 years. In other words the drink habit increased at the rate of about 7.5 per cent per year. The moral suasion of the temperance forces and the scientific teaching of public and private schools failed to stem the rising tide of inebriety.

The top panel of the graph on the opposite page shows the swing of the states to prohibition preceding the adoption of the Eighteenth Amendment. Maine was the first in 1851, then Kansas in 1880, and North Dakota in 1890. There were a number of other states which went dry in both of these "dry waves," but all except those named, went back wet either by popular or by judicial or legislative action. The third wave swept over the country beginning in 1907, carrying 30 states, which brought the total to 33 states to which should be added hundreds of counties and thousands of towns in the remaining 15 states.

The heavy line in the lower part of the graph shows the amount of tax paid liquor consumed in the nation beginning with only 4.08 gallons per capita in 1850 which vaulted to nearly 23 gallons in 1907—or more than five times the 1850 figure.

In 1907, on account of the increasing growth of local and state prohibition, this rapid upswing dropped from 22.66 gallons in 1914 under license to 2.48 gallons under prohibition—the lowest in the nation's history. There had always been bootleg and moonshine on the market, indicated by the broken line marked "estimated bootleg." Official estimates place the illegal traffic since repeal to be fully as great or greater than during prohibition. See pages 47, 60.

The shaded part of the graph shows the years that were under prohibition. The wavering lines stretching upward from 1920 to 1930 indicate the estimated amount of the illegal traffic during the dry decade from 1920 to 1930. The solid wavering line is the official estimate of the Department of Justice showing the "possible production of illegal liquor for the year ending June 30, 1930." This indicates the consumption of just over seven gallons per capita.

The broken wavering line is the estimate made in "The New Crusade," which is a wet propaganda handbook of facts and arguments to prove the failure of prohibition Their estimate was 1,100,000 gallons or 8.96 gallons per capita. (N2, p. 90) Therefore, by the wet admission prohibition reduced the national drink habit from 22.66 per capita in 1914 (wet) to 8.96 in 1930 (dry). Uncle Sam sobered up 50%! Moreover, his present rate of drinking is only 13.60 gallons. Uncle Sam was a hard drinker; but during thirteen years of prohibition, when he had to sneak out to the barn for his hootch, he tapered off to 8.96 gallons; and he is still drinking only 60% of his pre-prohibition intake.

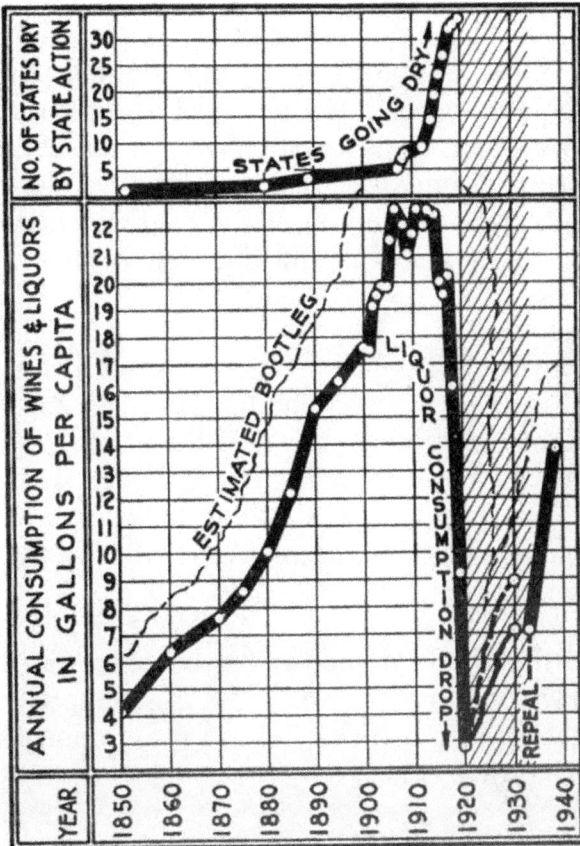

Mild measures of legal action such as local option and county option, while they had been effective locally, were not adequate to produce any measurable results on a national scale. As John G. Woolley, one of the most famous of temperance advocates of a few decades ago, used to say, "Local option is all right, except that it is too local and too optional."

States in which local prohibition had been tried, seeing the local benefit that grew out of it, started a veritable march for statewide prohibition in 1907. It had taken

more than a half century to secure the three dry states—
Maine, Kansas and North Dakota. During the next thirteen years, 30 states and the District of Columbia all
clambered onto the water wagon with "bone-dry" laws
prohibiting, in most cases, the manufacture, sale, importation, exportation, transportation and in many cases,
the possession of intoxicating liquor for beverage purposes. Consumption of intoxicating beverages dropped
like a plummet to below the all-time low record of the
nation's history.

This was a moral-political victory that probably has
no parallel in the history of the human race. A nation
of more than 100,000,000 reversed the political policy
of regulating the beverage liquor traffic, which is almost
as old as civilization, adopted total prohibition, and reduced the per capita consumpton from 22,81 to 2.48 gallons, or 89.1 per cent.

Look at the graph. It shows that the per capita consumption, which during the 64 years of attempted regulation shot up like a rocket, under prohibition came
down like the stick.

Q. What was the effect of this sudden decrease in the
consumption of alcohol throughout the nation?

A. The nation sobered up. The annual cost of the liquor traffic had been billions of dollars. The cost of taking care of the crime that resulted from it also ran into
giddy figures. The effect on the nation was very similar
to the effect upon a man who has been on a long debauch
and has sobered up and got the alcohol out of his system.
Moreover, national wealth improved greatly. Hence the
cost of sickness was greatly reduced. National income
went up by billions of dollars. The national death rate
sharply declined.

Our schools and colleges increased in attendance to a degree never before dreamed of. There was a great demand for labor and wages went up, and the number of strikes and labor disorders declined to levels that had not been known for years. The nation's per capita income bulged to figures far greater than ever known to this or any other nation. Our national debt was sharply reduced. Savings accounts mounted to all-time high levels. People invested in life insurance, business, stocks and bonds had a general distribution—not only among people that were called rich people but also among the great "middle class". There was a spectacular growth of industry of every kind.

While it would be unfair to say that Uncle Sam had been a sot or a depraved boozer, it would be true to say that he had been a steady and heavy drinker. He had suffered from all the evils that had come from over indulgence.

But he was drinking around 2,200,000,000 gallons per year (SA '22 p. 697) at a cost of over $2,000,000,000. That was about twice what he paid to send his children to school (ibid p. 104); ten times as much as he paid to send his young folks to college (ibid p. 109); over four times what he dropped in the collection plate at church (ibid p. 71); over ten times as much as much as he spent for roads and bridges (ibid p. 289); it was over three times all the dividends paid by the greatest railroad system on earth (ibid p. 317); twice the cost of his army and navy (ibid p. S96-S98); and almost as much as all the capital stock of all his national banks, (ibid p. S1S). Moreover, he spent a lot of time in jail for being drunk, disorderly and vagrant.

So he swore off, effective January 16, 1920. Then, as is always so in such cases, he began to behave better. He earned more money, hence had more to spend, wore better clothes, enjoyed better health, set a better table, had more money to send his children to school and college, invested more in his various industries, built more roads and made more improvements, and began to take more interest in culture—in the better things of life.

Here is the official record, taken from page 31 of the Census volume, "PRISONERS, 1923", (dry) comparing the record of that year with wet 1910, which shows how much better he behaved himself.

Offence Wet 1910	Dry 1923	% Decrease + Increase
Total - - - - - - - - - - - - 521.7	325.1	-37.7
Drunkenness - - - - - - - - - - 185.9	83.1	-55.3
Disorderly Conduct - - - - - - - 99.9	48.5	-51.5
Violating Liquor laws - - - - - - 8.4	35.8	+326.2
Vagerancy - - - - - - - - - - - - - 54.0	25.5	-52.8
Larceny - - - - - - - - - - - - - - 42.8	24.7	-42.3
Assult - - - - - - - - - - - - - -- -- 24.5	11.5	-53.1
Violating City Ordinances - - - 5.5	9.2	+67.3
Burglary - - - - - - - - - - - - --- -- 8.8	7.8	-11.4
Violating Drug Laws - - - - - -- 0.3	6.5	+2,066.7
Carrying Concealded Weapons - - - -- - - - - - - - - - - - -- - - - - - - - 7.0	5.1	-27.1
Fornication and Prostitution - 6.6	4.7	-28.8
Fraud - - - - - - - - - - - - - - - - - 9.7	4.3	-55.7
Forgery - - - - - - - - - - - - - - -- 2.2	3.7	+68.2
Homicide - - - - - - - - - - - - -- 3.1	3.6	+16.1
Gambling - - - - - - - - - - - -- 7.5	3.7	-50.7
Robbery - - - - - - - - - - - - - - 1.8	3.3	+83.3
Malacious Micheief and Trespassing - - - - - - - - - - - - - - - - - -10.9	3.4	-68.8
Non-support or Neglect of Family --- 3.0	3.3	+10.0
Rape - - - - - - - - - - - - - - - --- -- 1.5	2.0	+33.3
All Other Classified Offenses 26.5	15.6	-41.1
Unclassified ans Unknown -- 11.7	9.6	-17.9

Q. Are there other evidences that show that drunkenness was substantially and effectively reduced?

A. Yes.

The World Almanac for 1933, page 480, shows in

the wet and wicked City of New York arrests for drunkenness for the five wet years ending in 1916 averaged
47,690 whereas for the five dry years ending in 1931
the average was 19,314. This shows a decrease of 60.1
per cent. If allowance were made for increase of population the difference would be even more striking.
DRUNKENNESS IN N. Y. CITY

5 Wet Years

5 Dry Years

Every record, and even the admission of the professional wets, show a sharp decline in drunkenness.

Q. It has been claimed that more people suffered from
alcoholism during prohibition because the illicit liquor
was more poisonous. What are the facts?

A. The following table shows the percentage of alcoholic admissions as to the total admissions in the
Connecticut State Hospital from 1908 to 1929. The war
years—1918, 1919—are omitted as abnormal.

	All Admissions (Rate per 10,000 population)	All Admissions for Alcoholic Psychosis (Percent of total Admissions)
Year	Wet	
1908	4.7	14.5
1909	3.4	15.7
1910	3.3	16.0
1911	3.7	16.3
1912	3.1	20.0
1913	3.3	19.5
1914	3.8	18.7
1915	3.3	17.6
1916	4.0	15.7
1917	4.5	13.8
Average	3.71	16.78
	Dry	
1920	3.4	6.2
1921	4.1	7.3
1922	2.6	7.6
1923	2.5	6.3
1924	3.2	6.9
1925	2.9	7.0
1926	3.9	9.1
1927	3.9	8.9
1928	3.3	10.7
1929	3.1	9.4
Average	3.29	7.94

ALCOHOL PSYCHOSIS   (N.E. p. 242)

WET — 16.78%

DRY — 7.94%

Dr. Irving Fisher, professor of political economy at Yale, stated:

> "From all this, it is evident that the total consumption of alcohol today in beverage form is less than 16 per cent of pre-prohibition consumption and probably less than 10 per cent." (PW, p. 44)

Mr. Samuel Crowther, well-known writer on economics stated:

> "The actual amount spent for liquor today can hardly amount to more than half a billion dollars, but whether it be half a billion or a billion, the amount is paid for a volume of liquor certainly not exceeding 20 per cent of that sold in the pre-war trade. The wage earner who formerly frequented the saloon is not buying either in speakeasies or from bootleggers." (PP p. 57)

Herman Feldman, dean of the School of Business and Civic Administration of the College of the City of New York, and well-known economic counsellor and author, said:

> "As we see it, the wage earners are paying out a great deal less on drink and all that went with it than they did before prohibition, or than they would spend

today if we did not have prohibition .... It appears to us most likely that the great mass of the people, however, are spending much less on drink today than in pre-prohibition days." (AS p. 382)

That liquor is responsible for a very large proportion of crime is admitted by all students of the question. The Chicago Tribune, than which the liquor traffic has no more loyal and militant friend, said editorially:

"An overwhelmingly large proportion of the crimes against the person and property are due to the saloons. There it is that the bummers and vagrants, the thieves and the murderers are made. Men who would otherwise be decent, respectable, orderly members of society, earning their living with the sweat of their brow, get into the habit of going to these places, abandon labor, and, unable to pick up a living in any other way, resort to crime for it." (Quoted in Union Signal, 12-15-31)

Chicago is a typical American city. The commitments to the house of correction in that city for 1917 (wet) and 1921 (dry) were as follows:

Year	Male	Female	Total
1917 Wet	14,267	1,663	15,930
1921 Dry	8,081	485	8,566
Decrease	6,186	1,178	7,364
Percentage Decrease	43.3	70.8	46.2

Commitments to the Chicago city jails for the same year were as follows:

Offence	1917 Wet	1921 Dry	Decrease
Assult and Battery	73	47	26
Assault with Deadly Weapon	237	162	75
Breach of Peace	10,467	5,490	4,977
Cruelty to Animals	5	0	5
Gambling	47	13	34
Larceny	2,046	15,68	478
Adulterty and Fornication	65	24	41
Inmate House Ill-Fame	133	9	124
Soliciting to Prostitution	38	4	34
Wife and Child Abandonment	661	1	660
Totals	13,772	7,318	6,454

WET YEAR — 13,772

DRY YEAR 7,318

Dr. George Kirchwey is probably America's best known criminologist. He was Commissioner of Prison Reform for the State of New York, was warden of Sing Sing Prison, has been lecturer on criminology in many of the biggest and best universities and colleges, and a contributor to the Encyclopedia Britannica, etc. Discussing the effect of Prohibition on crime, he said:

"Let us take courage from the official record covering the eighteen years 1910 to 1927 inclusive, which shows a marked decline of from 35 to 40 per cent in the general crime rate in the United States, and this notwithstanding the immense number of new crimes, resulting from liquor, drug, and traffic laws enacted since 1910. That the offenses of assault, fraud, vagrancy, prostitution, and larceny, the last the most common of serious offenses, should all have fallen off by 50 per cent or more, and burglary by 10 per cent or more, should give pause to the Jeremiahs." (A-6-8-29)

The World Almanac for 1932 in the table at the bottom of page 553 shows arrests in New York City for homicide, for other felonies, and for intoxication as follows:

	Homicide	Other Felonies	Intoxica-tion	Population
1912 Wet	417	11,256	25,605	Average 5,136,706
1913 Wet	351	11,386	26,207	
1914 Wet	433	12,981	23,122	
1915 Wet	452	14,044	22,635	
1916 Wet	263	13,428	19,453	
Total	1916	63,195	117,022	
Average	383	12,619	23,404	
Per 100,000 Average Pop.	7.5	247.4	458.9	
1926 Dry	306	13,073	12,330	Average 6,017,702
1927 Dry	282	11,832	11,977	
1928 Dry	373	12,609	13,353	
1929 Dry	373	12,837	10,982	
1930 Dry	377	13,350	11,408	
Total	1711	63,701	60,050	
Average	342	12,740	12,010	
Per 100,000 Average Pop.	5.7	212.3	200.1	

These figures show that the per capita homicides were 31 per cent, other felonies 11 per cent, and intoxication 129'per cent greater during the wet years.

Judge Gemmill of Chicago, in a letter to Gifford Gordon of Australia on July 26, 1922, wrote:

".... In presiding daily over our criminal court, I find that those who are now arrested for drunkenness are generally old topers: those who have been hard drinkers throughout their entire adult life. We have very few young men brought into the court now on the charge of drunkenness, and it is very seldom that such young men are found anywhere in our city in an intoxicated condition .... I have found that what is true in Chicago is true in every other large city in America. There has been a decrease in the number of persons arrested in America for drunkenness of over 600,000 a year."

Q. Did the poisonous bootleg liquor sold under prohibition greatly increase the deaths from alcoholism?

A. No. The Vital Statistics of the United States show that during the five wet years, 1913-1917 inclusive, the rate of alcoholism deaths per 100,000 population was S.2S. Came prohibition, and the deaths from alcoholism dropped to 1.0 or a decrease of 80.8 per cent. For the dry years, 1920-1930 inclusive, the average rate was 3.10 or an annual saving of 1.95 per 100,000 population.

The graph below visualizes the facts. From 1913 to 1917, largely wet, the deaths from alcoholism averaged 5.25 per 100,000 population. Under war-time prohibition and rigid war-time restrictions the alcoholic death ratio dropped to 1, a figure far below the lowest in the records of the nation. Then there was an increase until 1928, after which there was a rapid decline to 2.50. Then came repeal and with it the decline was sharply halted with an immediate upward swing.

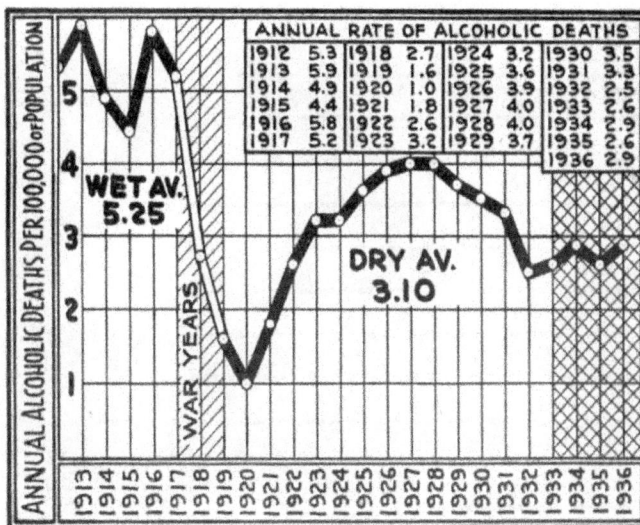

ANNUAL ALCOHOLIC DEATHS PER 100,000 OF POPULATION

ANNUAL RATE OF ALCOHOLIC DEATHS							
1912	5.3	1918	2.7	1924	3.2	1930	3.5
1913	5.9	1919	1.6	1925	3.6	1931	3.3
1914	4.9	1920	1.0	1926	3.9	1932	2.5
1915	4.4	1921	1.8	1927	4.0	1933	2.6
1916	5.8	1922	2.6	1928	4.0	1934	2.9
1917	5.2	1923	3.2	1929	3.7	1935	2.6
						1936	2.9

WET AV. 5.25

WAR YEARS

DRY AV. 3.10

The death rate from cirrhosis of the liver, a recognized alcoholic disease, was 12.3 prior to prohibition; since prohibition it is 7.6, showing a saving of 4.7 per 100,000 population. (WA 1933, p. 367.) Deaths from Bright's Disease, a recognized alcoholic disorder, per 100,000 population were 105.3 before prohibition; under prohibition 91.5, showing a saving of 13.8 per 100,000 population.

The average alcoholic death rate in dry 1930 was 3.5. But in the states which had repealed their prohibition enforcement acts the alcoholic death records were: New York, 6.4; Montana, 6.7; Massachusetts, 5.5; Maryland, 6.8; Rhode Island, 8.3 and Wisconsin, 3.6. Of these, Maryland never had an enforcement act, and Rhode Island was one of the two states which did not ratify the 18th Amendment, and her enforcement law was ineffective. The rate for these states averages 6.2 per 100,000 population, as against 3.5 in the nation. The rate in these wet states is 77.1 per cent higher than in the nation at large.

Average — 3.5

New York — 6.4

Montana — 6.7

Massachusetts — 5.5

Maryland —6.8

Rhode Island — 8.3

Wisconsin — 3.6

Q. Was there reliable evidence to show that there was any less drinking among children?

A. Much, though the wets often made unsupported assertions to the contrary. Judge Bartelme of Chicago, speaking from experience, said:

"In 1913, when I began to hear girls' cases, 8 or 10 per week were brought to me on the charge of intoxication. They have almost disappeared." (C. 7-7-28.)

Col. Amos W. W. Woodcock, who was formerly Commissioner of Prohibition, after investigation in 1930, officially reported that:

"There is less drinking by both girls and boys than before prohibition.

"There is less drinking in homes than before prohibition.

"There is less drinking at social gatherings attended by youths of high school age than before prohibition.

"A very small proportion of either high school boys or girls drink liquor at all, and the number of habitual drinkers is almost negligible. "The use of liquor does not in a large measure contribute to juvenile delinquency. "There is less juvenile delinquency.

"Conditions are not ideal, even though they now are far better than before the adoption of the Eighteenth Amendment."

Evangeline Booth who has spent her life for the redemption of the "down-and-outs" said:

"The children are ragged and emaciated representatives of the condition that has happily changed. 80 per cent of the suffering of the families of the common laborers of our city was wiped out by prohibition."

From Telegraph Hill, San Francisco, on the Pacific, to Massachusetts Bay on the Atlantic came the almost unbroken testimony from child welfare organizations that prohibition immensely improved the conditions of the under-privileged children of the nation. The Telegraph Hill Neighborhood Association in the vicinity of the old Barbary Coast vice district stated:

"Since the passage of the (18th) Amendment, the entire outward appearance of the neighborhood is changed. Previous to 1920, intoxication was very common. The boys stopped at the open saloon before coming to the dances and slipped out frequently during the evening for a drink .... Children used frequently to sit on the steps of the neighborhood house completely stupefied by the drinking of red wine .... After a careful investigation, we have decided that conditions in this neighborhood are 90 per cent better. (P5, p. 59)

Q. Did drinking in colleges increase under prohibition?

A. The records say not. In June, 1930, the Associated Press polled the college presidents to get information concerning drinking and drunkenness in the colleges. Two hundred and fifty-five replied and out of this number 237 reported either that there was no drinking or that there was less drinking than prior to prohibition. Only three reported that drinking conditions were worse under prohibition than before. Here are the figures:

3 reported drinking conditions worse under prohibition.

7 reported drinking among students "bad".

8 reported no change.

47 reported that drinking among students is unknown.
44 reported no drinking among students.

146 reported a decrease in drinking under prohibition.
255 total.

Dean H. E. Stone of the University of W. Va.:

"Every one of the older faculty members and citizens with whom I have talked is positive that conditions have improved as to the town and the University as to the prohibition law."

Nearly everyone admits that conditions in the smaller colleges are much better, but let's take some of the big ones.

For 25 years, Dr. T. A. Clark has been in the University of Illinois. He states:

"Drinking before prohibition was much more general than now. There was much more general drinking and much more drunkenness and it was much less talked about."

For 22 years Professor Charles C. Clark has been on the Committee of Discipline at Yale University. He says:

"I know conditions intimately. I do not pretend that the students are not drinking, but the change has been simply revolutionary. In the old days our Committee was constantly busy with cases involving intoxication and the disorders originating from it. Now we have practically no business of the kind at all to transact. Moreover, this is in spite of the fact that in the old days we rarely troubled ourselves about a case of mere intoxication if it had not resulted in some kind of public disorder, whereas now intoxication of itself is regarded as calling for the severest penalty."

For 30 years Dean Edmondson has been connected with the University of Indiana. This is his testimony:

"Drinking among students is much less than in former days. It is true that there is some drinking Most of it is done by visitors."

Q. Is it true that the average criminal was younger during prohibition?

A. No, although there are many reasons why this should be true. Probably no period in the world's history has seen crime played up in the news press and on the screen so spectacularly and attractively as during recent years. Children and young people respond to the glamor with which crime has been clothed. Moreover, home restraints are relaxed since the war. Yet the young commit a smaller proportion of crime under prohibition than formerly. The Children's Bureau of the United States Dept. of Labor so reports.

Clear official evidence is found in the Census report on prisoners, which shows a decline of 43 per cent in the commitments of offenders under 18. (PW, p. 71).

Another official report is that of Herbert C. Parsons, Massachusetts Commissioner of Probation, who states:

"The decrease in juvenile delinquency during the past ten years is due to prohibition .... There are other factors in the improvement, all of them taken together, not equalling, in my judgment, the effect of prohibition."

As further evidence of the effect of prohibition upon youth is the fact that "first-time convictions" for drunkennness in New York City dropped from 35.3 per 10,000 population in wet 1914 to 8.9 in dry 1919, a reduction of 74.7 per cent. (NE, p. 47)

The Massachusetts Society for the Prevention of Cruelty to Children reported "that prior to prohibition intemperance was present in the homes of 47.7 per cent of the families known to this society." Under prohibition the percentage dropped to 16.8 per cent in 1921, 20.2 per cent in 1922, 23.2 per cent in 1923, 21.9 per cent in 1924 and 18.9 per cent in 1925. (NE p. 48)

Q. Did the speakeasies, blindpiggers and bootleggers under prohibition sell as much liquor as the saloonkeepers did before?

A. No. Whiting Williams (WW), social investigator, who goes right out and lives with the working people months on end in order to get their viewpoint, worked in the steel plants in 1919 (wet) and returned for several months' work there as a laborer, incognito, in 1930 (dry). In his report of his experience, he said:

"The afternoon of that last summer day I was prepared to defend this conviction: All speakeasies in Homestead (Steel Mills) are not handling in a whole average day as much either of alcohol or money as crossed an average saloon bar in Homestead during a single morning of 1919. The reason is plain. The present-day workers' speakeasy lacks almost completely the well-known 'come hither'—the ancient lure—of the old saloon. The bright lights, the warmth, the good cheer and fellowship, the companionable chromos of well-built femininity, all these are missing. Instead, the speakeasy is likely to offer only the grime and darkness of a sloppy kitchen plus the furtiveness which makes everyone glance up quickly every time the door is opened to make sure that no law' has entered. Not by any stretch of the imagination can such a place be called 'the working men's club.'" (M June 21, 1931.)

Noted Wet Writer Testifies

The late Arthur Brisbane, said to have been the highest paid and most widely read feature writer of all time, was an avowed wet. He lived in New York City for nearly 50 years. He knew New York as Dickens knew London. Yet in 12 years under poorly enforced prohibition, Mr. Brisbane never saw a speakeasy, according to his statement in his syndicated column, "TODAY" of December 13, 1931. Nor did he see one even then until a friend showed him the way! The place, he wrote, appeared to be locked up. When they rang the door-bell, an eye peeked through a little diamond-shaped window to look them over; then the door opened; inside there was another inspection, strong locks then opened and they were let into a hidden den, similar to the old saloon-restaurant of bygone days.

But in the old days hundreds of such joints were running wide open blazoning their welcome with glittering signs to the veriest stranger. Their patrons numbered men and women, young and old, where the hidden joints operated behind double-locked doors would have only vouched-for guests.

The place that Mr. Brisbane was shown in New York he himself could not have found alone nor could he have gotten into it according to his own description without a sophisticated guide. Under license any boy or girl, man or woman, who was an utter stranger would have not only passed noisy, smelly saloons by the dozens in a short walk on any of New York's principal streets, but would also have passed "swell", saloon restaurants for the fashionable of both sexes which catered less to hunger and more to thirst.

There would have been bright lights, alluring music, neon signs, and should one have strolled over onto the Bowery, there would have been booze joints and hot spots with solicitors out on the streets enticing passers-by to enter. There he would have found every form of vice and crime with touts and "come hither" harpies beckoning the wayfarer to enter wide open doors.

The repeal of the 18th amendment has again opened up these gilded dens of destruction. Under prohibition they were hidden, accessible only to those who hunted them out or found some habitue who would show them the way and vouch for them.

Q. Was there intentional distortion of facts, for the purpose of arousing sentiment against the law?

A. It would seem so. At least here are a few illustrations. Mrs. Mabel Willebrandt in her book, "THE INSIDE OF PROHIBITION," writes, "An illustration of the mass of misinformation in current circulation, which served to hinder and delay a sane view of the liquor problem, is contained in a letter I received recently," and she appends a copy of a letter which reads, in part:

"Philadelphia, Pa.

"My dear Mrs. Willebrandt:

"Some time ago at a meeting of a board of directors in Philadelphia, a business man who is ordinarily keen and shrewd, said that he had heard that tremendous numbers of drunks were being taken weekly to the Hospital and that owing to the poisonous nature of the liquor a large percentage of deaths ensued; that the previous Monday morning there had been sixty dead bodies removed by the undertaker. He had heard this on apparently good authority and repeated it as credible. The yarn was so preposterous, however, that I thought it was worth while taking the trouble to run it down, so I addressed a communication to the superintendent of the Hospital, asking if it were true. I received the following letter in reply:

"'Dear Sir:

"In reply to yours of recent issue, state that we have had no deaths from alcoholism in two years. We looked up our records and upon investigation found that on October 10th, 1927, a man died of benzine poisoning which was first thought to be alcoholism.

"'Very   respectfully,   ,
" '_____ Hospital.' "

That is certainly a generous discount—from 60 deaths to none!

And here are others which are in point.

The Press "Makes Medicine" for Repeal

On the ninth day of June, 1929, a man was driving with his wife from the direction of Canada near International Falls in Minnesota. Two revenue officers not prohibition enforcement agents, seeing him coming, and thinking he might be bringing in contraband, strung their sign, "STOP," across the road. He slowed down his machine as though to stop. The officers dropped their stop sign and started toward the automobile. The driver, presumably thinking that with the drop of the sign he was given the right to go, stepped on the gas. The officers called loudly to him to stop. He kept on going, perhaps not hearing them. After he had passed and was driving away one of the officers shot to puncture the back tires of the car with a sawed-off shotgun. Unintentionally the man was killed. The news press screamed in big front page headlines from the Atlantic to the Pacific, condemning the act as a piece of mad prohibition fanaticism. The papers over the nation carried lurid news stories and angry editorials. The big dailies and news vending organizations sent staff representatives and photographers half way across the country to International Falls, and the subject was kept "hot" for days. Cartoons, condemning Uncle Sam for this act appeared from coast to coast. Prohibition and the Prohibition Enforcement were flailed mercilessly. The revenue officers were Called murderers and savages; and although they were not prohibition officers the public was led to believe that they were. In September, three months after the event, the Chicago Tribune and other papers warmed the whole thing over again in blistering editorials "making medicine" against prohibition.

Now here is a similar case but treated differently by the press. In October of the same year a grocery store a short way out from Cleveland, Ohio was robbed. In the morning a crowd of curiosity seekers gathered to view the scene. A man separated himself from the crowd and walked briskly away. "Halt!" shouted a policeman, and the man quite innocent of the fact that he was being called upon to stop walked on. The policeman called to him twice more; then he pulled his gun and shot him dead. The Cleveland papers gave the incident about seven inches on the front page but with an inconspicuous headline. This was not "big news." It could not be used to inflame sentiment against prohibition—Hence it might rate two inches in Chicago with probably no space in New York, Minneapolis or the Pacific Coast. Both incidents were practically identical with perhaps more blame attaching to the Ohio officer. The only real difference between the two was that the Minnesota incident could be twisted to deceive, and to inflame and anger the people of the United States against prohibition. It, therefore, was played big in all the papers over the United States, editorialized, cartooned, and headlined to the limit.

Here is another illustration:

Incident A. In 1928 a woman in Michigan was convicted of selling a schoolboy a bottle of gin. It was her fourth conviction of a felony, and she was sentenced under the mandatory "habitual criminal" law of the state to the penitentiary for life. The press of the nation stormed and shrieked at the "outrage" and wept copious tears over the law's brutality and demanded her pardon. All these efforts were ballyhooed in big space in the newspapers for weeks. "A Pint for a Life," was made a national slogan by the press. The case was blazoned in editorials, and by cartoons; and the stage was set for a spectacular drive for the repeal of the "habitual criminal" statute in the Michigan laws when the legislature next met. The whole story was warmed over again and featured with editorial anger and tears. Sentiment swept over the nation and telegrams were poured on the Michigan legislature in basketfuls from all over the Union. The law was repealed and thereafter the woman was pardoned. Perhaps that was well. But the press sobbed and shrieked its paid-for hatred of prohibition. It was faked sorrow and mock anger. It was sham sympathy for the habitual criminal. Its purpose was to inflame hatred for prohibition.

Incident B. In 1929, a man went into a Texas restaurant and, seeing 30c and-a pie on the counter near the door, he grabbed them and ran. He was caught, tried, convicted, and under the Texas law was sentenced for life as a habitual criminal. The two incidents are practically identical except that one could be used to fire the anger of the people against the alleged cruelty and bar-

barity of the prohibition law. The other could not. Ten years later it was found that the man who had stolen pie and 30c, was still doing his life term in the penitentiary, with no one to weep over him, no editorials to blame the government for sending him, for the small crime of stealing 30c and a pie, to serve the remainder of his life in the penitentiary.

Probably most news papers seek to print only legitimate news, keeping in mind proper perspective. But when the wets were willing to pay generously for poison gas attacks upon prohibition, an item which normally would rate an inch of space would be given 50 or even 10,000 inches, if it could be made into hatred or ridicule of the Eighteenth Amendment. And "there's a reason."

Children and Schools

Q. Did prohibition have any measurable effect on our public school system?

A. Our school system is generally considered the palladium of our liberty and progress. It has no foe that is so deadly as the liquor traffic, which robs the home of its money, its ambition, its culture and its character, and robs childhood and youth of a normal, wholesome environment. The record increase in registration and attendance in our public schools reveals the phenomenal stimulus of prohibition, and the decline of both as the tragic consequences of repeal.

The U. S. Office of Education reports that the increase in school attendance for the last five wet years preceding prohibition averaged 257,030 per year: for the first five dry years, the attendance jumped to 737,670 per year, a gain over the wet years of 187%!

Comparing the attendance in 1932, the last dry year of record, with 1936, the last available repeal yean an increase of attendance of only 53,423 for the four repeal years is shown.

This is an average increase of 13,356 per year or at the rate of only one fifth of one per cent per year.

Wet increase of 257,030 per year

Dry increase of 737,670 per year

Repeal increase of 13,356 per year

Now consider the teachers. From 1915 (wet) to 1920 there was an increase of 73,903 or an average of 14,751 per year for the five wet years. From 1920 to 1925 (dry) the increase was 99,741 or an average of 19,948 per year for the five dry years. In' 1932, the last dry year, the total number of teachers was 871,607. In 1936. the fourth repeal year, the total number of teachers had dropped to 870,963, showing an actual loss of 634 teachers per year for the repeal years as against an increase of 19,948 per dry year. (WA. 1940, p. 567.)

Now let us turn to the colleges where records must be given by decades. During the wet decade, 1910 to 1920, the attendance increased from 266,654 to 517,166, a gain of 250,512 or an average of 25>051 per year. In the next ten years, dry, the attendance mounted to 1,085,799 showing an increase of 568,633 or 56,863 per year—more than double the annual gain during the wet period.The records show but four repeal years, from 1932 to 1936, during which time the increase in attendance was only 53,644 or 13,411 per year. The annual increase during the dry years was more than four times as great as after repeal. (WA, 1940, p. 565)

Wet—increase of 25,051 per year

Dry—increase of 56,860 per year

Repeal—increase of 13,411 per year

The spectacular upswing of public school and college attendance immediately upon the closing of the saloon is unparalleled in this country. It is probably unapproached in the history of the world. Then came repeal, and this spectacular growth in school attendance dropped by 98%, and the increase in college attendance dropped to one-quarter of the prohibition level.

School Reports from the States

At the request of the Wickersham Commission, (WC) Dr. J. W. Crabtree, (WW) Secretary of the National Education Association, secured a report on truancy, delinquency, juvenile court cases, drinking and drunkenness, living conditions, attitude of students toward their studies, sports, and athletics, and the deportment of students at their social gatherings. Comparing the days before prohibition with the days since, the evidence was overwhelming that conditions were greatly improved under prohibition. The following condensed replies are typical:

ALABAMA—"There is less drinking at social gatherings of high school students now than there was in 1920."

CALIFORNIA—"Liquor drinking has not increased. Boastful talk on the part of a limited group has created a general impression that it is on the increase."

CONNECTICUT—"A. B. Meredith, commissioner of education of Connecticut, writes that the cases in which alcohol is evident are unknown to him."

IDAHO—"Many high school principals reported no cases of drinking for many years, many reported less than 4 per cent, and nearly all reported the situation far better than prior to the eighteenth amendment."

ILLINOIS—"Before prohibition the cases arose out of a genuine desire for intoxicating liquor, now the few cases observed are the result of a desire to appear 'socially smart.'"

INDIANA—"Before prohibition in their social gatherings, girls and boys would both be under the influence of liquor. The situation today is almost entirely free from this evil."

IOWA—"Today, while there is some drinking, it is not at all comparable to what it was before the days of prohibition."

KANSAS—"Since Kansas has had prohibition for a long time, it would not be possible to expect any improvement as the result of national prohibition."

MICHIGAN—"Evidence appears definite and consistent that truancy, use of alcoholic drinks, and delinquency of all kinds have been decreasing regularly and rapidly."

MINNESOTA—"Of the 15 educators who answered the

question as to the use of alcohol, 12 gave it as their opinion that there was less alcohol used by students."

MISSOURI—"Conduct at social gatherings, generally, is better; there may be some gatherings where intoxicants are used, but these are very few."

NEW HAMPSHIRE—"Ernest W. Butterfield, commissioner of education, writes that it is his impression that drunkenness , is very much less apparent than it was before prohibition.

NEW MEXICO—"There are fewer students drinking now than under former conditions and school children have less temptation now than they did when the saloons were open."

NEBRASKA—"A very small proportion of either high school boys or girls drink liquor at all and the number of habitual drinkers is almost negligible."

NEVADA—"Supt. Walter W. Andres Carson City, states that there is no record of any cases of use of alcohol by students brought to his attention or to his board."

OHIO—"Less use of alcohol by students, less truancy, and a better attitude toward sports and work."

SOUTH CAROLINA—"Prof. Harry Clark, dean of the Furman Summer School, writes that drinking is absolutely out at his college today, although there was a little drinking a few years ago."

TEXAS—E. B. Comstock, principal of the North Dallas High School, Dallas, Tex., reports "In our High Schools, generally speaking, there is no liquor problem. If a boy drinks at all, he drinks occasionally because he thinks it is smart."

UTAH—"Milton Bennion, dean of the school of education of the University of Utah believes that drinking is much less prevalent among young people now and that present conditions are much more favorable for education and training toward good citizenship."

VIRGINIA—"Miss Maude Glenn writes: "Prohibition has given an increased interest in clean sports and athletics."

WASHINGTON—"In matters of temperance, clean living, and morality, the standards among high school boys are at present very much higher than before prohibition."

WYOMING—"There is no question that the home conditions of the students are better and that parents are better able to send their children to school. "This evidence shows that young people of high school age are not drinking more, but less; that there has been an improvement in enrollment, attendance, conduct, and attitude toward work and play. No one can read this evidence and be anything but optimistic regarding American youth of high school age." (WC. pp. 63-81.)

Q. Did the teachers of our public schools in general support prohibition?

A. Yes. The National Education Association has passed many resolutions supporting prohibition since the adoption of the law and none against it.

Q. Did the Congress of Parents and Teachers approve prohibition?

A. It did. Here is its official declaration:

"We affirm our belief that the present Eighteenth Amendment is already a national benefit in curtailing the distribution and use of alcoholic beverages and we pledge our support to a thorough education of youth in homes and in schools as to the deleterious effects of alcoholic beverages and narcotic drugs upon health, working ability, and morals."

Moreover, it taught it in its educational literature.

Here is an example taken from one of its leaflets,

WHAT THE EIGHTEENTH AMENDMENT HAS HELPED AMERICA ACHIEVE

(1) The removal of the open saloon which encouraged gambling and degraded politics.

(2) The reduction of the amount of consumption of alcoholic beverages by seventy per cent within a remarkably short time.

(3) The elimination of liquor advertising which appealed to the crudest and lowest emotions to create new victims of the drinking habit.

(4) The protection of children and their mothers from the neglect and brutality of drinking fathers.

(5) An increase in savings that has given the common man and woman in America the highest economic and social position enjoyed anywhere in the world.

(6) The most efficient industry to be found anywhere because of the reliability and loyalty of sober working

men and women.

(7) The reduction of many forms of vice and crime until cities are safer for law observing citizens today than they have ever been.

(8) The moderation of "automobile" and "postwar" crime which would have created terrible conditions in a country with 25 million autos were liquor not outlawed

(9) The development of all types of schools so that millions of young people have a richer educational opportunity. High school enrollment alone in the United States increased from two million in 1920 to nearly five million in 1930—the most remarkable advance in the history of civilization.

(10) The foundation for a future rich in promise and opportunity for home life, for education, for government, for labor, for industry, and for the realization of religion.

Q. Do the beer halls and taverns affect young life directly? The Junior Protective Association of Chicago, in its leaflet on The Tavern and Community Life, says:

"The sale and use of liquor has always been one of the great social problems which challenged our efforts. Our reports, until the 18th Amendment was passed, bear evidence that liquor was one of the great contributing factors in dependency, delinquency, crime, broken homes and deteriorated neighborhoods, venereal disease and mental breakdown. * * *

"During the prohibition era we did not have many complaints which could be definietly related to the sale of liquor or to its use by minors. * * * Taverns (since repeal) not only have directly involved juve-

niles in situations which seriously affected their welfare, they have also had a demoralizing effect on the
entire community, * * * because of broken homes, domestic discord, neglected children and the increased
burdens heaped upon welfare agencies. Tavern con-
tributed to crime, deliquency, promiscuity and immorality."

Labor

Q. Does it take more labor and more material to make
beer than it does to make most other commodities?

A. No. Exactly the opposite is the fact. In a 1910 Census Bulletin when the breweries were operating at top
speed it was shown that when the consumer paid $100
for such things as automobiles, boots and shoes, cloth-
ing, furniture, leather goods, lumber, and other like
serviceable commodities, labor on the average received
$16.57; but when the consumer spent $100 for beer and
other intoxicants, labor received $7.63. Putting it anoth-
er way, when the consumer bought $100 worth of liquor,
labor lost $8.94—the difference between the $16.57 paid
to labor for useful commodities and the $7.63 paid labor
for making intoxicants.

Labor's Share of $100 Worth of Booze

Labor's Share of $100 Worth of Goods

And the producer of raw material suffers worse.
When the consumer spends $100 for the useful articles
named, the producer of the raw material receives $58.73,
but when the consumer spends his $100 for liquor the
producer of materials receives only $23.49. Otherwise

stated, when the consumer spent his $100 for liquor, the producer of raw materials lost $36.24. These are authoritative government figures, gathered in a wholly impartial survey.

Producer's Share of $100 Worth of Booze

G o o d s

Q. Did prohibition bring a reduction of wages?

A. No. Dean Edward T. Divine of the American University, in an article in the August, 1932 Current History showed by the wage index that the purchasing power of wages increased from 102 in 1914 (wet) to 260 in 1927 (dry); under prohibition actual wages more than doubled. Good wages spell prosperity. Prohibition pays.

Wages 1914 — Wet

Wages 1927 Dry

Taking another slant: The Statistical Abstract for 1939 on page 772 shows that industrial wages for all industries in 1914 (wet) were $4,076,719,000 whereas in 1929 (dry) the total industrial wages aggregated $11,684,476,000— Almost three times as much.

The table shows that in 1914 (wet) there were 7,023,865 industrial wage earners, whereas in 1929 (dry) there were «,836,402—an increase of 1,836,402.

Q. Is there evidence that labor conditions were affected by prohibition?

A. Yes. The figures seem to be conclusive. The Monthly Labor Review for May, 1939, page 1112 shows the number of strikes and the number of men that were involved for the years 1916 to 1937 inclusive. During the four years prior to prohibition there was an average of 3,805 strikes per year involving over two million men annually. Here are the figures:

STRIKES—During wet years before prohibition

Year	Number of Strikes	Men Involved
1916	3,789	1,599,917
1917	4,450	1,227,254
1918	3,353	1,239,989
1919	3,630	
Total	15,219	8,227,508
Average	3,805	2,056,877

STRIKES—During Dry Years

Year	Number of Strikes	Men Involved

1920	3,411	1,463,054
1921	2,385	1,099,247
1923	1,553	756,584
1924	1,249	644,641
1925	1,301	428,416
1926	1,035	329,592
1927	707	329,939
1928	644	314,210
1929	921	288,572
1930	637	182,975
1931	810	341,817
1932	841	324,210
1933	1,695	(Beer Legalized) 1,168,272
Total	17,189	7,680,529
Average Per Year	1,227	548,609

—Monthly Labor Review; May, 1939; p. 1112
(For figures under Repeal, see page 65)

During the thirteen years of prohibition the number of strikes dropped to an average of 1,227, or less than one-third as many labor disputes and less than one-sixth the number of men involved per year during the dry years when men were not squandering their money for liquor.

3805 strikes per WET year

1,227 strikes per DRY year

2.056.788 men involved per WET year

548,609 men involved per DRY year

For wet years AFTER prohibition see page 65)

Q. Did Prohibition bring the depression?

A. The depression was world-wide. It came to the European countries first and worst. Every civilized country suffered grievously from it. Prohibition promotes prosperity. And here is proof.

Taking 1914 as a typical wet year, and 1931, after the United States had more than a decade of Prohibition, there is conclusive evidence that under Prohibition the country attained levels of prosperity unequalled in the nation's history. The growth and expansion of business surpassed all precedent. Here is a table as it was published in the press in 1932 showing the expansion Of business under prohibition:

	1914 Wet	1931 Dry	Gain
Volume of Trade	22 Billions	40 Billions	82%
Bank Deposits	19 Billions	52 Billions	178%
In Savings Banks	9 Billions	28 Billions	211%
National Income	36 Billions	70 Billions	48%
New Life Insurance	12 Billions	16 Billions	33%
Average Income Per Capita	$360	$562	56%

(Detroit News, quoted in Christian Science Monitor, February 18, 1932)

And here is further proof: In 1932 under Prohibition, the United States

had 7% of the world's population, but it

wore 37% of the world's cotton;

and 39% of the world's shoes;

and had 40% of the world's highways;

and burned 42% of the world's coal;

and used 44% of the world's copper;

and used half of the world's electric energy;

and half of the world's paper;

and 53% of the world's iron;

and 57% of the world's steel;

and 61% of the world's timber;

and burned 72% of the world's petroleum;

and drove 83% of the world's automobiles.

To credit Prohibition with all of these gains would be unfair; but, just as a man who wastes his time and money for drink saves less, has less, enjoys less and develops less because drink from the very beginning dulls his mind, reduces his earning capacity, and makes him less efficient and less dependable; so a nation will suffer economically and socially in proportion as the people drink. Under Prohibition Uncle Sam out-stripped the drinking nations of the world.

Q. Was prohibition responsible for heavy losses and grave evils in the Industrial world?

A. No. The Wickersham Commission investigated the matter and stated that under prohibition the industrial benefits include: "Increased production, increased efficiency of labor, elimination of blue Mondays, decrease in demands on charity and social agencies." (Wickersham Report, Doc. No. 722, p. 71.)

Q. Did national prohibition increase the average income of the nation?

A. Undoubtedly it did. "A sober man makes more, spends more, saves more and enjoys more." Nearly everybody has seen that proverb proven. Since a nation is made up of men, it would be clear that a sober nation would make more, spend more, save more and enjoy more than a nation which is half drunk. Anyway, here are the figures.

Year	Per Capita income	Year	Per Capita income	Year	Per Capita income
1910	Wet - - - - - - - $305	1920	dry - - - - - - - $642	1933	wet - - - - - - - - $356
1911	" - - - - - - -- 300	1921	" - - - - - -- 524	1934	" - - - - - -- 407
1912	" - - - - - - -- 309	1922	" - - - - - -- 520	1935	" - - - - - -- 441
1913	" - - - - - - -- 326	1923	" - - - - - -- 589	1936	" - - - - - -- 508
1914	" - - - - - - -- 319	1924	" - - - - - -- 592	1937	" - - - - - -- 537
1915	" - - - - - - -- 327	1925	" - - - - - -- 610	1938	" - - - - - -- 478
1916	moist 384	1926	" - - - - - -- 631		
1917	" - - - - - - -- 454	1927	" - - - - - -- 626		
1918	drying 550	1928	" - - - - - -- 633		
1919	" - - - - - - -- 599	1929	" - - - - - -- 654		
		1930	" - - - - - -- 588		
		1931	" - - - - - -- 485		
		1932	" - - - - - -- 374		
Average - - - - - - - - $387.30		Average - - - - - - - - $574.40		Average - - - - - - - - $454.50	

Average For Pre-Prohibition Years

Average For Prohibition Years

Average For Post-Prohibition Years

LIFE INSURANCE

Q. What about life insurance? It is a good yard stick by which to measure the social security of the home.

A. For the seven years preceding prohibition, the average annual amount of new life insurance purchased per year in the United States was $2,716,000,000. Here is the record:

NEW LIFE INSURANCE WRITTEN IN U. S. A. For the Seven Years Preceding Prohibition	
Year	Amount
1913 -	$1,840,000,000
1914 -	1,826,000,000
1915 -	1,928,000,000
1916 -	2,362,000,000
1917 -	2,892,000,000
1918 -	2,965,000,000
1919 -	5,199,000,000
Average Per year - - - - - - - - - - - - - -	$2,716,000,000
(Spectator Insurance Index, August 20, 1940)	

For the thirteen years of prohibition, the annual average amounted to $10,987,489,000—an increase of 304%. New business exceeded $14,000,000,000 during these successive years. This was an evidence of prosperity and of social security for the average American family never before approached. These figures tell the story:

NEW LIFE INSURANCE WRITTEN IN U. S. A. For the Thirteen Years During Prohibition	
1920 -	$7,079,449,000
1921 -	6,787,343,731
1922 -	7,506,249,499
1923 -	9,454,634,329
1924 -	10,151,898,447
1925 -	11,816,746,801
1926 -	12,412,621,104
1927 -	12,670,848,675
1928 -	14,168,100,848
1929 -	14,529,157,975
1930 -	14,159,712,274
1931 -	12,379,144,571
1932 -	9,721,456,059
Average Per Year - - - - - - - - - - - - - -	$10,987,489,461

Agriculture

Q. Is it true that the breweries and distilleries would use an immense proportion of the grain produced thus exerting a strong influence upon the grain market?

A. No. It is true that the wets usually make that claim. However, on May 7, 1917, wet, the Evening Star, of Washington, D. C. carried the brewers' own testimony showing the insignificant amount of grain that the brewers consumed. Here is the report:

"Headed by Gustav Pabst a delegation representing the brewers of the United States was heard today by the Senate agriculture committee on Senator Gronna's bill to forbid the manufacture of grain into alcoholic liquors during the war.

"The actual amount of grain used in brewing, principally barley, they told the committee, represents less than threequarters of one per cent of all the grain produced in the United States, and in addition to that, the barley used, they said, is not a staple human food, here or abroad.

"From these figures the brewers argued that the brewing industry was too small a factor to be considered in the food conservation program."

Q. Would that small percentage of the total favorably affect the price, not of grain, but of all other farm commodities?

A. No. Minneapolis is the market for the great north central grain belt of the U. S. and Winnipeg is the market on the Canadian side. As to transportation facilities and local and international markets they are on equal footing.

The Chicago Tribune of Nov. 2. 1930 in an editorial captioned "PITY THE CANADIAN FARMER" deplored the fact that barley was selling in Winnipeg at less than 26c a bushel. Winnipeg had plenty of breweries and so had the entire Dominion of Canada which, according to the theory of the wets, should have supported the barley market.

At the same time barley was selling in Minneapolis, which had no operating breweries nor had the rest of the United States, at from 48c to 54c per bushel. If, as has been claimed, the brewery supports the barley market, these prices should have been reversed.

Again, the Minneapolis Journal of October 27, 1932 published this table showing the price on the same day of farm commodities in Winnipeg and in the Twin Cities.

Commodity	Winnipeg	Twin Cities	TwinCities Advantage
Wheat	48 1/4c	55c to 58c	17.1%
Flax	72 1/2c	$1.11 to $1.15	54.5%
Beef Steers	$4.50 to $4.75	$6.50 to $8.75	39.3%
Lams	$4.00	$5.00 to $5.50	31.3%
Butter	19c	22c	15.8%
Eggs	15c	22c	46.6%

The farmers in wet Canada found their markets are very substantially below the markets in dry U. S. A. At the same time, they find their dollar at a substantial discount in the markets of the world as compared with the U. S. dollar.

Q. Did the prices of grain go up or down immediately following the adoption of national prohibition?

A. They went up. Mr. Louis J. Taber, head of the National Grange, which is the largest organization of farmers in the nation, showed by the records of the agricultural department that in the hey-day of the liquor business, wartime years excluded, corn averaged 59c per bushel, while under the first nine years of prohibition, the price averaged 72c; for the wet years rye averaged from 39c to 68c; during the first nine prohibition years it averaged from 65c to $1.20 a bushel. The per capita consumption of sugar in the U. S. jumped from 87.9 lbs. per capita to 116 lbs.; and the consumption of milk went from 42 gallons per capita to almost 60 gallons per capita; the consumption of cheese increased 50% and the consumption of butter 24%, a gain of 31%; and the consumption of milk went from 42 gallons per capita to almost 60 gallons per capita, an increase of 30%.

Q. Do not the farmers demand the legalization of the manufacture of liquor as a relief measure?

A. No. Congressman Clifford R. Hope of Kansas, in a speech appearing in the Congressional Record for April 29, 1932, said in part:

"I represent one of the greatest grain-growing districts in the country.

"It is a singular thing in all the discussion we have had of beer as a farm-relief measure none of it has come from farmers or those representing' farmers. Recently the Committee on Manufacturers in the Senate held extensive hearings upon the proposal to legalize beer. The report comprises some 574 pages.

"More than 50 witnesses testified in favor of the measure. Many predicted their advocacy of it on the theory that the manufacture of beer would be of great benefit to agriculture. Yet not one of the witnesses so testifying was a farmer or representative of a farm organization. Among the witnesses were numerous Members of Congress. They too, stated that beer would help the farmer. Yet, not one of these Members represented a strictly rural district. On the contrary, they were from. Detroit, St. Louis, Buffalo, New York, Chicago, Peoria, and Seattle.

"During all the time I have been in Congress I have been a member of the Committee on Agriculture. I am acquainted with the legislative representatives of all the farm organizations in the country. They have been assiduously working here in Washington for legislation which their organizations believe will be of benefit to agriculture. Yet I have never heard of any representative of these organizations advocating beer."

A columnist, writing in the Minneapolis Journal on March 28, 1933, said:

"Any talk about the new 3.2 beer being 'slop' is silly. It will have just about the same 'kick' as the average pre-prohibition light beer and will be about the same as the present Canadian beers, so far as alcoholic content is concerned."

THE FAMILY

The Wickersham (WW) Commission (WC) was set up by President Hoover for the purpose of investigating the workings of Prohibition. Nearly all of its members were known as "wet" or indifferent, with only one a pronounced "dry." Their investigation which resulted in a five volume report upheld Prohibition as very salutary and beneficial socially and economically. A special sub-committee on "Opinions of Social Workers in Family Welfare Agencies," in submitting its report stated: (WC)

"In most cases these replies are based on discussion by the executive of the organization with his entire professional staff, frequently supplemented by consultation with other social workers of the city, school-teachers, judges, policemen, and others whose opinions would be valuable."

The sub-committee reached the following conclusions:

1. That intemperance is a much less important factor as a cause of economic dependence than it was before prohibition . . .

2. That on the whole there is less drunkenness in evidence now than before prohibition in the homes of workingmen and on the streets and in other public places . . .

3. That the standard of living among workingmen's families as measured by material comforts, has improved noticeably . . .

4. That there is less neglect of children by their mothers in consequence of intemperance, less cruelty to children, and less brutal treatment of wives, and that the quality of family life among the poor has thus benefited from prohibition . . .

5. That the prevailing attitude of people toward the liquor laws, as observed by our correspondents, is either indifference or defiance.

6. That the illegal manufacture and sale of intoxicating beverage is common among the families in the stratum of society known to relief organizations . . .

7. That this illegal traffic has a very demoralizing effect on those who are engaged in it, especially on the children of the household.

Among many general observations were the following:

There is a general agreement, though with a few exceptions and a number of qualifying comments, that intemperance is a much less frequent factor among families applying for relief than it was before prohibition. "Formerly," as one puts it, "drunkenness was taken for granted; now it is regarded as a problem." "The eighteenth amendment," writes another, "has completely changed the character of our work." Another says: "We do not come across the family where a week's earning has been squandered at the saloon; where the man is unable to report for duty Monday morning; where the family furniture has been broken up and the dishes smashed; the children afraid of their father, and the mother very much discouraged."

Organizations which have useful case records, extending over the period under discussion, say that before prohibition intemperance was a major factor in 15, 26, and 48 per cent, even as high as 60 per cent of the families under their care. Several give figures showing that this proportion dropped to as low as 1 or 2 per cent soon after the legislation went into effect; but that after that it rose again, and in recent years has fluctuated between 7 and 10 per cent, one mentioning 13 per cent for the current month . . .

One of the large relief agencies in New York comments that, in the recent industrial depression, the problem of unemployment has not been complicated by the serious intemperance which accompanied similar depressions in 1914 and 1915, and to even a greater extent, earlier depressions. Unemployment is bad enough at best, but when complicated with drinking the difficulty of dealing with the family situation is far more serious.

As a conclusion of the investigation the sub-committee states:

"Most of the writers think that prohibition has been a factor in raising the standard of living since, as one of them puts it, the abolition of the saloon has made it possible for many weak-willed men to reach home on pay day with their earnings; and, as another observes, quite a bit of money that was spent for liquor it now spent for gasoline. One declares that prohibition with all its faults has raised the standard of living among the underprivileged to an almost unbelievable height." (WC pp. 310-es.)

General Evangeline Booth, of the Salvation Army probably knows the family life of the under privileged better than any other. She speaks from a long and intimate knowledge of the devastating curse of alcohol in the home, and of the redemptive influence of prohibition, even in the Bowery, that world-famed Gehenna of New York's notorious East Side.

"In New York, before prohibition, the Salvation Army would collect 1200 to 1300 drunkards in a single night and seek to reclaim them. Prohibition immediately reduced this gathering to 400. . . . Our report from the Bowery is that drinking in that difficult area has dropped 60 per cent—that is, to less than half what it was . . . "The people who advocate regulation have short memories. They do not seem to be aware that it was the failure of regulation throughout the United States that drove us into prohibition. Nor is there any country in the world where regulation has solved the liquor problem. In the United States it was regulation which corrupted our politics, bribed our law courts and maintained our red-light areas.

"The Bowery was notorious for more than 100 years as the great crime center of the metropolis, if not the country. Under the licensed saloon the gangster organizations were thoroughly entrenched; concert halls and gambling clubs of a most vicious character were doing business in a high-handed way. Many men were murdered in cold blood and buried beneath the buildings or thrown into the sewers or otherwise done away with . . .

"There was much bootlegging going on in the days of the saloon—more than in these days. The Bowery and Third Avenue was a veritable hell on earth from the vice and brawls that went on not only with the gangsters and the tough boys of the neighborhood but many families as well. What a wonderful change has been brought about in a reign of quietness for the neighborhood since prohibition came!" (N. Y. Times. Apr. 27, 1930)

The Congressional Record of May 18, 1932 carried a letter, from George H. Davis, head of the Salvation Army in Chicago which states:

"Among more than a million poor and unemployed with whom we have come Into direct contact in the past sixteen months in the Chicago district alone we find that under prohibition the evidence of drink as a factor has been reduced to the vanishing point."

Lillian D. Wald in charge of a Henry St. Settlement of New York City says:

"I have no hesitation whatsoever in asserting that prohibition despite its weakness has worked untold good to the greater part of our population. * * * No longer do we see the hideous alcoholic wrecks who a few years ago patronized the bread line."

Albert J. Kennedy, well known social worker, author and lecturer, writing in the April, 1933, SURVEY GRAPHIC says:

"Three months after the saloon closed its doors, working class communities right across the country seemed to have been absolutely remade. The half drunken gangs of youths and boys that used to lounge on the street corners disappeared. I have not seen a woman drunk upon the streets since 1920. The quality and quantity of drunkenness in the highways and in the street cars decreased to less than 1 per cent of the pre-Volstead Days. * * * There has been no poverty under the present depression comparable to the old type of liquor poverty. * * * A heavy proportion of men and a great many women were completely sober. Every dance and party, every political rally, most trade unions and lodge meetings got under way in a slightly maudlin manner. There was always a proportion of 17, 18 and 19 year old boys who were beginning to go the way of their fathers."

Q. Jane Addams of Hull House, Chicago, knew the actual results of Prohibition at first hand. What was her testimony?

A. "Here around Hull House we used to watch whiskey and beer being left at saloons by the drayload. The poverty and suffering from drink was appalling. There Is such a difference now that it seems like another world. Our poor are moving away into better places. The whole standard of life is rising for them. Drinking has decreased, and so has our work of rehabilitating families wrecked through intemperance. We have hardly any more squalid homes and neglected families to deal with. The stuff folks get now makes them uglier, but its evils are offest by the difficulties of getting it. I would not see the old system again for anything."

"So long as the greatest single crime cause—Intoxicating liquor—is permitted, protected, and to a great extent promoted by government, crime in this country will continue to be as deadly and as costly as war." (Senator Morris Sheppard, excerpt from speech before U. S. Senate, 1-16-40.)

Q. Did prohibition sharply improve the economic status of labor?

A. In his book, Prohibition and Prosperity, Mr. Samuel Crowther, the well-known economic writer and authority, answers that question most conclusively. By the generous courtesy of The Ladies' Home Journal and Mr. Crowther some excerpts of the findings of that thorough survey follow:

Mr. E. J. Buffington, then president of the Illinois Steel Corporation of Gary, Indiana, says:

"With the absence of saloons it is certain that workingmen are now spending far less money for drink than before prohibition . . . ." (p. 28)

A. R. Erskine, president of the Studebaker Corporation in the same wet district, writes:

"Our workmen are spending not only less money for drink than before prohibition, but are spending practically no money for drink." (p. 29)

The Thompson Wire Company, with plants at Boston and Worcester, said:

"My opinion is that the workmen are spending far less money for drink than before prohibition." (p. 29)

The Newport Rolling Mill Company at Newport, Kentucky, said:

"Several years ago we opened up a bank near our plant and from the number of accounts, both saving and Christmas saving, we are convinced that the money that was formerly spent in a saloon is being laid away as savings." (p. 30)

R. H. Scott, president of the Reo Motor Car Company writes:

"Workmen are spending a very small percentage of their wages for drink as compared with the saloon days." (p. 36)

Charles Piez, chairman of the Link-Belt Company, had an investigation made through the foremen of the various plants which resulted in this characteristic report:

"It is the firm conviction of these men that our workmen are spending less than in days before prohibition. We seem to have no 'after pay-day' or 'after holiday' problem. There is every evidence of greater interest in saving accounts, and without question the workers' families have more to spend now and are living much better.

"Since prohibition there is an increase in number of home owners, a far greater interest in savings accounts and stock ownership." (p. 37)

Harvey S. Firestone writes from Akron—which used to be a very wet town:

"There can be no doubt that workmen are spending much less for drink, as a group, than before prohibition." (p. 38)

A. B. Bryant, president of the First National Bank of Gardner, Massachusetts, says:

"There is not the slightest question that the amount of money expended by workmen for liquor in this community is negligible at the present time compared with that before prohibition took effect." (p. 40)

Ralph H. Burnside, presid3nt of the Willapa Lumber Company of Portland, Oregon, says:

"The evidence appears incontrovertible that workmen are spending only a small fraction of the money they did for drink before prohibition." (p. 45)

George M. Verity, president of the American Rolling Mill Company at Middletown, Ohio, and with large

mines and mills elsewhere, had a survey made by foremen living close to the workers who were able to

"cite innumerable instances of men who are valuable employees to-day but who were excessive users
of alcohol prior to prohibition . . . The situation today has been changed altogether in that these men
now own or are paying on homes, own automobiles
and many other present-day conveniences . . .

"We certainly cannot overlook the fact that the
result of prohibition has been definitely reflected in
our business, since a large percentage of our product
is going into the manufacture of automobiles, refrigerators, domestic electrical appliances, radios, and
many other articles of this kind."

Here is a striking account of conditions in West Vir-
ginia, from Josiah Keely, president of the Cabin Creek
Consolidated Coal Company:

"I live right among miners and know personally
scores of hard drinkers who have almost quit drinking . . . The pay-day 'lay-off when saloons were here
was a rather serious interruption of business, both on
account of the absence and on account of the 'day after' headaches. The families are saving more and they
are undoubtedly enjoying a period of greater spending—for automobiles, radios, washing machines,
electric refrigerators, phonographs, etc ..." (p. 33)

Pickands, Mather & Company reports:

"We know that not as much money is spent for
drink as previously. We do not have the spectacle of
the mother coming to the office in tears and despair
because the father has gone out on pay-day night and
boozed the entire pay check." (p. 34)

Mr. E. J. Buffington, then president of the Illinois Steel Corporation of Gary, Indiana, wrote:

"Evidences of the economic value of prohibition are found in records of increased savings accounts and in the higher plane of living conditions of workingmen In general." (p. 27)

From Canton, H. W. Hoover says:

"Workmen are spending but a fractional part of the money they previously spent for drink. The dollars that were previously spent in saloons are now diverted to the more legitimate channels of merchandise, in which a much higher percentage of labor is involved." (p. 38)

From W. C. Dunlap, vice-president of the American Multigraph Sales Company, Cleveland, comes this:

"Our workmen are spending less money for drink than before prohibition. They own more automobiles, have larger savings accounts and have more cash in their pockets than they did before prohibition ..." (p. 39)

From very wet Buffalo, William H. Crosby, president of the Crosby Company, writes:

"The impression of our people is that there has been a great deal less drinking among our men since prohibition and a great deal more money to spend for other purposes. The streets around our plant are lined with motor cars owned by our workmen." (p. 42)

From Salt Lake City, E. O. Howard, president of Walker Brothers, Bankers, writes:

"A union representative advised me that workmen are certainly spending less money for drink than before prohibition, and for this reason living conditions are better, the majority of them own their homes and a great percentage ride automobiles to and from their places of business." (p. 42)

The president of the Canton Cotton Mills at Canton, Georgia, says:

"Our workmen spend practically nothing for drink since prohibition. It would be hard to compare these conditions in our community now with what they were before prohibition." (p. 42)

Donald Comer of the Avondale Mills, which employs five thousand people in five different communities, and has been operating since 1897, says:

"We are now spending less for drink than before prohibition. The outside and inside of the homes are in no way comparable to what they were in the old days. People are buying more and better furniture, cabinet victrolas, and radios, and automobiles are no longer uncommon, and everywhere . there is more regard for personal appearance ..." (p. 44)

There is an almost inexhaustible volume of testimony from welfare and social betterment organizations extolling the benefits of prohibition.

These illuminating quotations give but a fragmentary idea of the economic, social, cultural and moral benefits that prohibition brought to the nation. The losses that came with repeal in all fields of human activity are beyond computation—in many ways beyond comprehension.

"Therefore," concludes Mr. Crowther, "one of the objectives of the Prohibition Amendment has been achieved—liquor has been put out of the reach of those least able to buy it. The. minimum sums which are being diverted from the saloon into the buying of goods or into savings accounts are enough to account for a large measure of our prosperity. They are, in effect, new purchasing power—as has been explained. And since buying begets production, and production begets wages and profits, and these wages and profits beget more buying; we have an explanation of at least a part of the remarkable increase in buying which has taken place since Prohibition.

"Enforcement at the outside costs about forty million dollars a year. That is a direct debit to Prohibition. But the amount is negligible as compared to the direct benefits through the diverting of expenditures from liquor to goods and savings. Of course, on top of this comes the graft and crime and all that which is said to be directly traceable to Prohibition. This is undoubtedly very large indeed, but it is hard to believe that it approaches the old liquor graft.

"The saloon has always been the center of graft and crime, but while once we took this for granted, now a certain horror is affected at the graft and crime surrounding the bootleg traffic. Some of the bootlegger fortunes that turn up are large, but they do not approach the size of the fortunes left by many politicians and local bosses who were closely allied with the liquor trade. Today we have no local governments absolutely dominated by the saloon—and we used to have plenty of them. And many people choose to forget that the laws governing the old saloons were in most places framed solely with the thought of permitting them to be violated by paying graft. In New York City, for instance, the Prohibition laws are better enforced today than were the old Sunday closing laws.

"In saloon property the country over, there has been no loss at all. The old locations have been very generally taken over by chain stores or restaurants which do more business and employ more men than the saloons did. This does not apply to some of the very large saloons, but the number of these was small and most of them were in hotels.

The hotel business has distinctly prospered with the elimination of the bar—although the old timers could not accustom themselves to the change.

"In an investigation made of three thousand saloon properties in New York City, it was found that new businesses were occupying all of them, and the new concerns employed an average of between three and one-half to four and one-half men as against two men each for the saloons.

"The present debit side of Prohibition narrows down to the cost of enforcement—which is slight. The nuisance of enforcement is another matter.

"By the re-routing of at least two-thirds of the money which formerly went for drink into the buying of useful goods, a higher level of general living has been established in this country. This higher level has brought higher wages and still higher levels of living.

"We have as a nation been infinitely more prosperous since Prohibition than ever before. We are definitely going forward.

It would seem that Prohibition is fundamental to our prosperity—that it is the greatest blow which has ever struck, poverty

"I have examined, one by one, the other possible causes and have been forced to eliminate them. I have gone into the positive evidence of the bearing of Prohibition upon prosperity. The facts are inescapable. Prohibition is an economic success.

"The country is spending more than it ever did, but it is not spending recklessly; people insist on getting value. There is a keen desire to work. That which we have has come gradually and appears to be sustained by a new and steady force that we never had before.

"That new and steady force is undoubtedly Prohibition, but as a force it has been almost wholly concealed by the emotional attention which has been given to other phases of the law. The outstanding fact of Prohibition is that, by diverting expenditures from drink, it has made the country prosperous. That is the only fact which seems to be getting no considered attention.

"Every figure of wealth that we know has steadily climbed. The index value of sales in the department stores has gone from 87 in 1921 to 108 in 1928 and in mail order houses from 67 to 137. In 1919 we had only two thousand electrical refrigerators, and in 1938 we had nearly a million and a quarter. During the same period, washing machines ran from less than a million a year to around six million.

".... In 1919 there were around eighteen million individual savings accounts to a total of thirteen billion dollars. Last year there were more than fifty-three million accounts holding in them twenty-eight and a half billion dollars. In the building and loan associations, representing for the most part ownership of homes of moderate price, there were in 1919 somewhat over four million members, while in 1927 there were more than eleven million members."

After repeal, Joseph H. Choate, Jr., the head alcohol administrator, was quoted in the press to the effect that:

> "The bootleggers are now turning out from their stills alone, not counting smuggling and alcohol-divertings, a quantity of spirits which cannot be much less, and may be more than we drank before prohibition. This quantity is being consumed in addition to the entire sales of legal goods, which, ever since repeal, have run not far below pre-prohibition figures." (AS p. 51.)

IGNOBLE GREED

A SAD AND SORDID STORY

Q. What was the chief cause of repeal?

A. The chief—probably the only—cause for repeal was the Association Against the Prohibition Amendment (AAPA) which was organized eight months before the Amendment became effective. Its constitution declared:

"This Association has two immediate aims: (1) To prevent the country from going on a bone-dry basis on July 1, and (2) To make the Eighteenth Amendment forever in-operative."

It was organized to resist the enforcement of law. To deceive the public it hypocritically prated about its interest in "true" temperance, and falsely boasted that it accepted ho financial help from the liquor interests, and persistently blazoned its pretended opposition to the return of the saloon. Its blatant hypocracy was revealed when their list of contributors, filed in Washington under provision of the law, showed, among others, the following champions (?) of the Constitution.

Pennsylvania Central Brewing Company. Loewer's Gambrinus Brewing Company, The Garden City Brewery, The Buffalo Brewing Company, The Superior Beverage Company, Flock's Brewing Company, The Erie Brewing Company, The Lion Brewery, The Schaefer Brewing Company, Jacob Ruppert (Brewer), Gottfried Krueger Brewing Company, The Joseph Hensler Brewing Company, California State Brewers' Association, F. & M. Schaefer Brewing Company, Fred Pabst (Brewer), George Ehret, Jr., W. Fred Annheuser, R. A. Huber, care of Anheuser-Busch Company, Patterson Brewing and

Malting Company, Chr. Heinrich Brewing Company, Daeufer-Liederman Brewing Company, L. F. Neweiler's Sons (Brewers), Hugh F. Fox (secretary, U. S. Brewers' Association), William Hamm (Brewer), William Peter Brewing Corporation, Reno Brewing Company, Anheuser-Busch, Inc., Francis Perot & Sons Malting Company, Union Brewing Company, New York Malt Roasting Company, Philip Schneider Brewing Company, Froedlert Grain & Malting Company. (AS p. 6)

The Wisconsin Makers' Club also took a hand in raising money for the AAPA. Here is a copy of a letter they sent to their members:

Gentlemen: In view of the fact that the Wisconsin division of the Association Against the Prohibition Amendment has done such wonderful work during the last primaries, having been positively instrumental in securing eight wet out of the ten congressional candidates, and all of which facts were again praised and confirmed by Mr. Dietrichs of Chicago, at our meeting held yesterday, it was unanimously decided to give them further financial aid. (AS p7)

Q. Why did the multimillionaires fight prohibition so vigorously?

A. When talking among themselves they openly confessed that their purpose was to shift their taxes onto labor. They raised their campaign money on that appeal. In sending out a plea for funds Captain Stayton, organizer of the Association Against the Prohibition Amendment quoted Irenee Du Pont to the effect that if beer should come back with a 3c-a-glass tax he (duPont) would save ten million dollars in taxes on one of his corporations. (H2 pp 4165-6). The record revealed that this tax-dodging appeal went to rich men who were paying $100,000 or more income tax. (H2-p 4164). The argument was that they would profit by contributing to repeal as a means to reduce their taxes. Their plan was to exempt their corporations and incomes from taxes by shifting the burden onto beer drinkers. The memo, continues:

"If taxes should be taken off corporations, there would , be a rise in stock values and all owners of stock would profit accordingly." (H2^ p. 4165.)

Arguing further that large taxes would be raised from the working man, the memorandum says:

"The working men and others would willingly pay a tax of 3c per glass and at that amount would enable the Federal Government to get rid of the burdensome corporation taxes and income taxes, and to take the snoopers and spies out of offices and homes." (H2. pp. 4164-6.)

That plainly tells in blunt, brutal language the reason they wanted beer back—not to promote temperance, or to safeguard youth, or to crush bootlegging, or for personal liberty—but to shift the just taxes from their opulent corporations onto the burdened back of labor. In private they harped on only one string—evading taxes.

The Association Against the Prohibition Amendment reported to Congress that it spent $364,544 in 1932. Of this amount, Lammot Du Pont, of Delaware, gave $55,000; Irenee Du Pont, $32,000, and Pierre S. Du Pont, $57,000, or a total of $144,000. So, the wealthy Du Ponts contributed between a third and a half of the whole amount raised to fight the Constitution of the country that had protected them while they amassed billions. And their one and only concern was to escape the just taxes on those bloated billions.

Repeal was "put over" by a few fabulously rich men for the purpose of loading their taxes onto the under privileged working class.

It would be unpardonable to make that statement without the absolute proof of it. A memorandum of Captain W. H. Stayton, the organizer and moving spirit of the Association Against the Prohibition Amendment, contains the statement, verified under oath,

> "If we should have back the right to manufacture beer, if we should manufacture just as much as we did in 1914, and if we should tax it at the British rate, the income would be $1,320,000,000 or more than the amount received from income and corporation taxes. If the tax should be taken off the corporations, there would be a rise in stock values, and all owners of stock would profit accordingly." (H2. 4165)

Here is the air-tight proof that the motive back of the campaign for the repeal of the Eighteenth Amendment and the restoration of beer was to shift the taxes off the fabulous profits of the rich corporations and the multi-millionaires onto the craving of drinkers, chiefly workingmen with modest incomes. It will be noticed that the quotation definitely names "workingmen."

Here is further sworn evidence from the same report—Irenee Du Pont's statement

> "that one of his corporations would save $10,000,000 in corporation taxes if we should have, say, the British tax on beer."

This makes doubly sure the fact that the drive for repeal originated in the love of money, which is the root of all evil.

The plan originated in the mind of Big Money; the campaign was paid for by Big Money; the financial gain which Big Money achieved (if any) was at the expense of the moral, social and economic loss and degradation of the nation. Repeal was the result of a mendacious propaganda machine which continually told the people of the United States by every means known to modern publicity that good was bad, that truth was false and that lies were "gospel." Nor was the press, particularly the great daily press of the cities, guiltless.

The AAPA with its great wealth organized their own youth groups into a wet organization which was called the Crusaders. Among the leaders were Charles H. Sabin, Jr., son of the treasurer of the AAPA; Lamont Du Pont, III., of the Du Pont munitions and chemical empire which was probably more active in the AAPA than any other commercial or financial group.

The women presented a more difficult problem. Great national women's organizations such as the General Federation of Women's Clubs, the Young Women's Christian Association, the National Congress of Parents and Teachers, the National Women's Temperance Law Enforcement League, the Woman's Christian Temperance Union, the Lend-a-Hand Society, the International Order of King's Daughters, the Council of Women for Home Missions, and other like social, civic and church organizations were solidly for the Prohibition Amendment. The General Federation of Women's Clubs adopted the following:

"BE IT RESOLVED, that the General Federation of Women's Clubs, through its delegate body, reaffirms its conviction that prohibition offers the best means for curbing the liquor traffic and its attendant crimes and pledges its continued support to the Eigh-

teenth Amendment and the rigid enforcement there-
of." (AS. p. 114.)

Mrs. Henry W. Peabody, president of the Women's
National Law Enforcement Commission, estimated that
there were twelve millions of members in these organizations favorable to the 18th Amendment. This was a hard
nut to crack even for the chiefs of the AAPA. But they had
the money—by their own statement, forty billions of dollars. "Money talks" and these greedy plutocrats felt that
this was the time to make it speak its piece.

The Sabin family again went to bat to give "the labor-
ing men and others" their inalienable right to drink beer
for the express purpose of paying the just taxes of the
sordid plutocrats. So Mrs. Charles H. Sabin, wife of the
treasurer of the AAPA and mother of Charles H. Sabin,
Jr., of the young wet Crusaders, was elected president
of the Women's Organization for National Prohibition
Reform, of which Mrs. Pierre S. Du Pont, Mrs. August
Belmont, Mrs. John Sloane, Mrs. Coffin Van Rensselaer,
Mrs. Joseph Cudahy, Mrs. J. Roland Harriman, Mrs.
Henry B. Joy, and the wives of other multi-millionaires
were members.

These women alone could have made prohibition an
unqualified success. They chose instead to lend their time
and talents to its defeat by treating the law with blatant
contempt and flaunting its violation ostentatiously on
every occasion. They made lawlessness a mark of social
distinction and crime against the Constitution a badge of
"tax-exempt patriotism."

"If these women had been sincere, they would have
issued a statement as follows: 'We have our bootleggers,
we help finance the gangsters and racketeers of the un-

derworld, we serve cocktails and champagne at our brilliant social functions in the presence of our children, our servants and social inferiors; we hold the law in contempt and by our attitude, our talk and our conduct, we are helping to destroy respect for law. Although because of our wealth and influence we can obtain all the liquor we want in spite of the law, we want it repealed so that our husbands may be relieved of their income and corporation taxes.'" (AS p. 106.)

Thus the "malefactors of great wealth" trained their youth to trample on any law which lays a fair tax upon their swollen wealth; they also taught their women publicly to flaunt the flag in the holy cause of tax evasion—and it worked.

This women's organization went the limit in weeping over youth and bewailing the evils of intemperance which, they falsely asserted, was the out-growth of prohibition. To convince the world of their devotion to high and womanly aspirations and of their deep love for the temperance cause, and the youth of the nation, they passed the following resolution in April, 1932:

"BE IT RESOLVED: that this organization pledge itself to remain intact, directing its energy to the promotion of laws in the several states which will promote real temperance." (AS. p. 118.)

BUT

In September, 1933, when repeal was assured, and need for pretending that they were motivated by devotion to temperance and moral ideals was past, they brazenly flung aside the hypocrisy of concern for youth in the following resolution:

"BE IT THEREFORE RESOLVED: by the national executive committee that when the thirty-sixth state shall have ratified the Twenty-first Amendment, the national chairman be authorized to announce public-ly that, the aim of the Women's Organization for Na-tional Prohibition Reform having been attained, the organization thereupon be dissolved . . . ." (AS p. 119.)

This was an honest resolution. Having done their bit in the great, moral crusade (?) to transfer the just tax-es from the bloated fortunes of their husbands onto the "working men and others", they laid their armor down and kissed their beloved (?) cause of "real temperance" in final farewell.

Q. But was the fight for repeal in reality a crusade to reduce taxes?

A. Franklin D. Roosevelt was inaugurated as Pres-ident on the fourth of March, 1933, and on the twen-ty-fourth day of May the Associated Press sent a dispatch from Washington of which this a part:

"The Roosevelt administration today gave anoth-er shoulder punch to the movement for repeal, with Postmaster-General Farley declaring that unless the Eighteenth Amendment is written off the books ev-ery income taxpayer will have to hand the govern-ment $6 to $10 out of every $100 he earns this year .... He estimated that the increases would affect from 4,000,000 to 6,900,000 taxpayers this year."

Mr. Farley announced according to this dispatch that every democratic worker in the country would be urged to work for repeal on the ground that the bill providing for these added taxes had within it a definite provision that in the event that prohibition was repealed certain of these taxes were to be omitted.

For the first time in American history an open bribe was dangled before the taxpayers to vote for a law in order to shift the cost of government off the shoulders of the rich and onto the drink habit of "workingmen and others". And to win the votes of the low income group, the taxes on low incomes were raised and the law provided that if repeal were carried, the increase would be cancelled.

The AAPA had boasted and protested most emphatically that the purpose of the organization was to promote true temperance. As soon as the amendment was repealed, they forgot all this pious sham of "true temperance". To quote Fletcher Dobyns in his epochal, *"The Amazing Story of Repeal"*:

> "With absolute cynicism they demanded that no restrictions be put upon the liquor traffic, that the saloon be restored, and that private greed be left free to promote the sale of liquor and foster excessive drinking by every means that it could devise." (p. 99.)

As soon as repeal was achieved, Jouett Shouse, president of the AAPA, threw discretion to the winds and tore off the mask of pretended respectability and said in a speech:

> "I know the views of Mr. Choate with reference to the methods that should be pursued. I know his desire to make the industry self-controlling with the least possible measure of governmental interference .... knowing his fixed belief that the industry should be permitted to regulate itself with the least possible interference by the government .... he will strive in

every way in his power to make the application of the codes as little objectionable (to the "trade") as is possible." (AS p. 100.)

Q. Was there organized, systematic effort to manufacture wet propaganda?

A. There was. Here are a few of the many examples. Professor Peter Odegard, in his book THE AMERICAN MIND, published by Columbia University Press said:

"A prominent wet member of Congress once told the writer the principle upon which the wets base their propaganda:Every time a crime is committed, they cry "prohibition!" Every time a girl or boy goes wrong, they shout "prohibition!" Every time a policeman or politician is accused of corruption, they scream "prohibition!" As a result, they are gradually building up in the public mind the impression that prohibition is a major cause of all the sins of society."

In an article that appeared in VANITY FAIR, an aggressively wet magazine, Mr. Corey Ford, a well-known wet protagonist, said:

"Personally, I should like to call on every free-thinking American of my generation, and every American of the older generation who can think at all, to break this law; break it repeatedly, break it whenever he can. Drink what you please, when you please. Urge others to drink. Don't betray the bootleggers who are smuggling liquor for you. In every way possible flaunt your defiance of the Eighteenth Amendment. Render it inoperative; ignore it, abrogate it, wipe it out. While it stands, let it be disobeyed."

In one of their campaign booklets, called THE PRO-HIBITION PRIMER, the wets closed their argument with the statement.

> "So now you see how important, and even patriotic it is to disobey prohibition."

Theodore Roosevelt, when editor of the OUTLOOK, wrote:

> "The sources of information are choked by the daily press. * * * As many worthy citizens are almost wholly unaware (of this), they are naturally misled as to the rights and wrongs of any issue as to which the big interests deem it expedient that they should be misinformed."

Propaganda! That tells the story! Prohibition had achieved actual results by reducing the consumption of alcohol to less than a quarter of the per capita quota for 1914. It had reduced crime, lengthened the span of life, and brought on a period of prosperity never before approached in the nation's history. But the billionaires saw the possibility of loading the legitimate taxes on their bloated fortunes onto the back of labor, and propaganda turned the trick.

SINCE REPEAL

A *United Press Dispatch* recently carried an urgent appeal of Sanford Bates, director of Federal Prisons, calling for more new federal jails. He stated that from June 30, 1934, to June 30, 1935, the first full year under repeal, the federal prison population had increased 25 per cent. (Wash. U.P. Dispatch in Minneapolis Star, 1-4-36). "The relief which we expected from the repeal of prohibition," said Mr. Bates, "did not materialize".

The number of prisoners in federal institutions on June 30, 1935 (repeal) was 1,000 higher than the previous all-time high.

During the fiscal year ending June 30, 1935, the population of federal penal institutions increased from 12,201 to 15,417, said to be the largest increase of any year in the nation's history. (M. 2-1-36)

Here is the record of inmates in the City of Washington, D.C., comparing 1932, (dry) with 1936 (repeal) for fiscal years ending June 30. (Police Record).

Crime	(Dry) 1932	(Wet) 1936	% Increase
Felonies (Men)	3,624	4,850	33.8%
Felonies (Women)	131	419	219.9%
All Crimes	100,775	144,771*	44.6%
Drunkenness	15,315	19126	24.8%
* All time High			

The American Prison Association in its recent convention in Chicago stated that in the last year there has been an increase of 6,000 in prison population, with an all time high of 152,000 inmates. The total cost of crimes to the people of the United States has been frequently reported at 15 billion dollars per year by J. Edgar Hoover, Chief of the FBI. That is a staggering total which would pay our colossal national debt in three years. Alcohol is responsible for a large proportion of this crime.

Media Records, a leading advertising publication, estimates the total consumption of intoxicating beverages in 1937 at 1,939,869,030 gallons and estimates the cost at $3,602,555,706, which would mean $29.35 per capita including men. women and children.

This includes tax-paid liquor only. To find the actual total, there must be added the cost of a large amount of non-taxpaid liquors peddled by bootleggers and sold by the legal and the illegal trade. Joseph H. Choate, jr., while acting as Director of Federal Alcohol Administration, stated that

"the bootleggers are now turning out from their stills alone, not counting smuggling and alcohol-divertings, a quantity of spirits which cannot be much less, and may be more than we drank before prohibition. This quantity is being consumed in addition to the entire sales of legal goods, which, ever since repeal, have run not far below pre-prohibition figures."

Dr. W. A. Sturgess of the Distilled Spirits Institute recently stated that "every legal distillery in the United States has at least 100 illegal competitors producing bootleg."

The 1922 Statistical Abstract shows that the consumption of tax-paid distilled liquor for several years preceding repeal averaged about 138,000,000 gal-

lons, which, according to Mr. Choate, is the probable quantity of bootleg on the market today.
On page 2,685 of the Temporary National Economic
Committee's Hearings the consumer cost of bottled and
bonded whisky is shown to be $3.79 per quart or $15.16
per gallon. Counting the retail cost of bootleg at only $10
per gallon, this would add $1,380,000,000 to the annual
retail cost making a total of $4,982,555,706 or $38.26
per capita for tax-paid and bootleg liquor.

This computation of cost is conservative. It is based
on the usual retail price of 10c for twelve ounces of beer;
whereas, a large quantity is sold in exclusive bars at 15c
and a considerable amount at 20c, 25c, and even 50c a
bottle in the "gyp joints" and "swank" sporting spots.
These high prices in certain places apply to hard liquors
as well as to the beer. Considering these facts, the Methodist Board of Temperance calculates the retail cost at
$4,691,835,957, exclusive of bootleg and moonshine. It
would seem, therefore, that the $4,982,555,706 as com-
puted above, including the illicit as well as the legal consumption, errs, if at all, on the conservative side.

By way of visualizing this huge amount: it would pay
the cost of all public and private education, including all
elementary and secondary schools, normal and teachers'
colleges, universities and professional schools which to-
tals $2,630,826,000. (SA, 1939p. 108.)

In addition to this it would pay the total expenses of
all churches of all denominations in the United States
aggregating $817,214,000. (Ibid, p. 71.)

And to that may be added the annual pensions,
compensations, insurance and officers' retirement
pay for veterans of the World War and the hospital
and domiciliary care of the veterans of all our wars,

the total of which is $629,830,000. (Ibid, p. 151.) There would still be enough to

1.—Pay off all the small home mortgages under FHA, $473,246,000

2.—Pay all the unemployment compensation 396,400,000

3.—Cover the student aid under the National Youth Administration for six months 13,715,000

4.—Pay all the expenses of the American Red Cross for 1939 10,359,000

5.—Support the dependent children of all the states 8,968,000

6.—Cover the cost of aid for the blind 1,666-000

7.—And there would remain for trifling emergencies 331,706 SA, 1939—(1) p. 271; (2) p. 356; (3) p. 350; (4) p. 150; (5) p. 362; (6) p. 362.

The Association Against the Prohibition Amendment, a fanatically wet organization, made a study of drunkenness indicating that the rate per 10,000 population under license for three years preceding the war was 187.69 and that under prohibition since the War the rate was 126.37, a decline of 32.67 per cent. This is the ultra wet admission. (MT. p. 21.)

The 1923 Census report states that in 1910 (wet) 10.1 per cent of the admissions to hospitals were suffering from alcoholic psychoses, but that in 1922, (dry) three years after the Volstead Act, the percentage had dropped to 3.7 per cent. The report further said:

"The decline has been brought about by a change In the habits of the people with respect to drinking, and by the eighteenth amendment and laws prohibiting the manufacture and sale of alcoholic beverages." (NE. p. 99)

Even in the cosmopolitan City of New York records show that during wet 1912 to 1916, the average number of arrests for intoxication per year was 23,404 but in the same city during the dry years 1926 to 1930 the average annual arrests for drunkennes was 12,010—that means a decrease in New York City of 48.6 per cent in arrests for drunkenness comparing the dry years with the wet.

Prior to prohibition, the "graduates" from the Keeley Institute, a famous inebriate hospital, published a paper called "The Banner of Gold" which listed 123 branch Keeley Cures in the United States. By 1932, under prohibition, all but fourteen of these branches closed for lack of patients. Before prohibition there was also a chain of over 100 Neal and over 50 Gatlin drink institutes, none of which survived the drouth. In the State of Minnesota there were eleven inebriate hospitals, all but two of which succumbed in the long dry spell.

Immediately after the Civil War there was established in Chicago an institution for the care of inebriates called the Washingtonian Home. As the city grew, the Home grew. It enlarged its buildings, equipment and activities. In 1916 (wet) the Home cared for 1,114 inebriates; in 1920, the first year of Prohibition, the number dropped to 172; and shortly after this institution, which had been active for 56 years, closed its doors and sold its property for lack of drunkards! Prohibition was responsible for that.

Q. What about health?

A. Life insurance companies keep very comprehensive records and know the number of people that are rejected on account of ill health. Taking just the one item of rejection because of impairment of health by drinking, we find that after two years of repeal the number of applicants under age 30 which were rejected because of health impairment by alcohol jumped from 8.2 per hundred applications to 22.6, or an increase of 178 per cent. Alcohol is a poison, and its habitual or occasional use impairs health. The Annals of the American Academy of Political and Social Science in September, 1932, submitted actuarial tables showing that, taking total abstainers as a standard at 100, deaths among temperate drinkers were 142, and deaths among moderate steady drinkers were 212.

BOOTLEGGING

Repealists loudly proclaimed that repeal would abolish bootleggers, blindpiggers and other like racketeers. But these criminals prospered after repeal. The official organ of the wets whined:

> "A horde of bootleggers yet remains to harass enforcement officials, to undermine and discredit the legal liquor industry, to foster crime and rackets, and to rob the country of millions in evaded taxes." (Repeal Review).

The Chicago Daily News, discussing post-prohibition conditions, says:

> "The saloon is back, liquor is in politics, bootlegging continues, drinking has increased, unemployment is worse, and the cost of fighting the illicit trade is still burdensome."

The Federal Government had every reason to do its dead level best to stop bootlegging. The chief cry of the repealists was, "Banish the bootleggers and blindpiggers." Since these outlaws pay no revenue, the Federal Government hates them and goes the limit to eliminate the non-taxpaying traffic. A big type paragraph over a news story hi the United States News of July 13, 1936, says:

> "With repeal it was hoped that the bootlegger would go, but Uncle Sam's battle to put him out of business continues on a large scale with increased federal forces thrown into the fray."

During the old prohibition days there was much whining and no small amount of profanity on the part of the wets because the Government employed 2,500 special agents to fight the bootleggers. That was the peak number under prohibition, but after repeal the Government added 2,000 more special agents almost doubling the force after prohibition. Business Week one of the leading business journals, said:

> "Despite claims from Washington that bootlegging has diminished to a 'mere trickle' realists estimate that 40 per cent of the national consumption Is still from illicit sources."

To check upon the evidence of liquor law violation from a news standpoint, a count was made of all news items dealing with blindpiggers and other liquor law violations in the Minneapolis Star. For the month of July, 1932, under prohibition there were 35 column inches devoted to liquor lawlessness; but during July, 1938, two years and a half after repeal, 61 inches were required to tell the story of bootlegging, blindpigging, and moonshining. In other words, liquor lawlessness nearly doubled under repeal.

On January 20, 1935 (wet), the Minneapolis Journal in a leading, illustrated article captioned "More Stills Operating in Minnesota Than Before Repeal" gave facts and figures, names, dates and places proving that bootleggers and moonshiners operate more freely and safely under regulation than under prohibition.

Q. Has drunkenness decreased since repeal?

A. No. The records show a sharp increase. In Washington, D.C., arrests for drunkenness increased 48 per cent, comparing 1932, before repeal with 1935. Women drunks increased 53.6 per cent. The press recently stated that orders had been given to the police not to arrest drunks unless they were disorderly. In Los Angeles the official records show that in dry 1926 there were 2,700 arrests for drunkenness. Ten years later under repeal the number had increased to 56,000 or an increase of 1,974 per cent.

A news item in the Washington Star describing the situation says:

"Women drunks swamp police—riff raff, also debutantes, college girls in their 'teens, women of wealth and social leaders."

Since that date Washington has established a spacious farm for inebriates with a capacity for 200 drunks per day.

Minnesota state inebriate farm had 224 inmates during 1932 (before repeal). In 1935 (repeal) there were 385, an increase of 71.8 per cent.

The State Hospital for the Insane at Fergus Falls, Minnesota, reports that alcoholic admissions increased 300 per cent the first year of repeal.

A news item in the New York Times stated, "Alcohol admissions to Bellevue Hospital are increasing by leaps and bounds."

And the Boston Globe of November 21, 1936, three years after repeal, said:

"With alcoholism increased to such an extent .... that it is the greatest and most expensive problem in the city hospital"

Q. What about youth since repeal?

A. Because of their inexperience and because 3.2 has been falsely advertised as non-intoxicating, the probability is that youth suffers more from repeal than adults. Dr. Alice Aldrich, superintendent of Chicago Welfare Association, states in her report for the first year after repeal that:

"Chicago present-day saloons are causing delinquency among young girls to an extent never equalled, even in the old days. Young people of opposite sexes drink openly until they are no longer responsible for their acts .... The saloons with their back room and upstairs facilities constitute an alarming cause of immorality."

Jessie F. Binford, director of the Juvenile Protective Association of Chicago, depicted youthful depravity as the result of repeal, saying:

"The nudity of female performers serve to lure trade for the liquor resorts . . . Smutty jests of entertainers, filthy songs, and skits of indecent dialogue and licentious gestures appear in all parts of the city. Little Children are pressed into service .... Boys and girls under age are patrons .... The dance hall girls are shockingly young, some in their middle 'teens. The character of the dancing in these places was a revolting orgy of sexuality of the lowest order."

The St. Paul Daily News in a lurid story of the new saloon, said:

"There were three bartenders and a number of young barmaids serving drinks. Present were many girls who could not have been more than 16 or 17. Some appeared about 14. Liquors were served to youngsters of any age. No questions were asked .... Girls who earlier in the evening looked chic and neat, became bleary-eyed. Vile stories were told aloud. The dancing became obscene .... Such places abound in St. Paul."

Such places also abound in road houses out beyond police control in roadside nooks, by the highways and in many villages and small cities. They reach into the high schools and even into the grades for their prey.

Dr. William Healy, noted professor and specialist of mental diseases and lecturer in Yale and Harvard Universities says in his book, The Individual Delinquent:

"The effect of a little wine or beer upon an adolescent girl in breaking down her normal social and moral inhibitions is notorious. The effect is produced by premeditation of companions of both sexes who desire to lower the intended victim's levels of behavior. Many well founded social studies of the connection between drinking in dance halls and saloons and beginning prostitution are now available. One of the most simple and direct is to be found in the report of the Vice Commission of Chicago. In our own study of cases, we have learned the facts over and over again;

and they amount to just this: There was a desire for company and pleasure on the part of the girl; even in bad company there would be resistance to the many suggestive influences thrown about her, except for the directly decisive part played by a physio-psycho-logical condition with the use of liquor to which she was unaccustomed, a feeling of not caring possessed her, and the step was taken."

On the twelfth of February, 1934, a little more than a year after repeal, the Los Angeles Times reprinted part of a report of a school investigator to the superintendent of schools in which he "declared conditions to be appalling and said his investigations indicated that at least 30 per cent of the patrons of beer and wine parlors are under 21 years of age."

One of the investigators harked back to the license days and stated that "he never saw such conditions and characterized the present outlook as dangerous in the extreme." In the same year three of the leading newspapers in Chicago made an investigation in that city. The Herald-Examiner for March 6, 1934, carries a typical report:

> "Shocking evidence of how Chicago's high school girls and boys—children ranging between 13 and 18 years of age— are being lured into depravity by plying child patrons with liquor has been .... discovered during a fortnight's survey of the city's unregulated saloons .... Orgies which outrivaled the debauches of Paris' notorious Quartier Latin Drunkenness and laxity of morals are common in the dimly lit back rooms of these saloons, many of which carry on their vicious trade in the very shadows of the city's schools.

> "Sprawled on the floor and asleep at the long tables were a dozen boys and nearly as many girls.

Some were obviously 14 and 15 years old. The older ones were 17 and 18. These children were students at Lake View school ....

"A blonde child of about 16 is dancing for the crowd at the bar. Her skirts are to her hips. She is drunk .... They're raffling off a pint of bonded whisky for a dime a chance .... a 16-year-old girl screams with pleasure when she wins it. . . ."

Dr. Alice Phillips Aldrich welfare superintendent of the Illinois Vigilance Association, declared:

"The ancient and blood-stained commerce in agonized souls of girls has been revived since the return of the licensed taverns and promiscuous drinking between sexes .... As now operated, many so-called taverns have a most deplorable effect on girls. Nothing like it on so open and broad a scale was heard of in the days when the segregated vice districts were in full blast .... It doesn't make much difference whether there are bars or counters, stools or tables, whether sandwiches are served or not, or whether the drinking is done perpendicularly, the effect is the same."

A year later, the Chicago Juvenile Protective Association reported:

"No provision of the law is more disregarded than the article banning the sale of intoxicating liquors to drunken patrons."

"Vice in Chicago's saloon-taverns flourished. Some saloons are simply houses of prostitution, having adjacent rooms used for vice; hostesses solicited at the bars and tables, thence repairing to connecting quarters with the patrons. In other cases, streetwalkers came into the saloons to solicit . . . Cab drivers routed their fares from the liquor resorts to the houses of ill fame "(AS p. 193.)

Frank G. Fitzgerald, the Governor of Michigan, said:

"The situation today with respect to the legalized liquor traffic is worse than it was in the darkest days of the saloon .... The beer and liquor joint with its windows obscured, its lights dimmed, its booths to afford privacy—-with a dance floor as one adjunct and tourist facilities as another—is a combination as vicious as any that has ever been devised to debauch the morals of a rising generation." (AS p. 194.)

An editorial in the Chicago Daily News portrayed the results of repeal graphically as follows:

"Repeal was urged by its sanguine supporters as the remedy for all the ills of the dry regime .... None of the promises has been fulfilled. The saloon is back, liquor is in politics, bootlegging continues, drinking has increased, unemployment is worse, the revenue returns to the state treasury are far below the hopeful estimate of 1933, and the cost of fighting the illicit trade is still burdensome." (AS p. 196/)

LABOR

STRIKES During Wet Years After Prohibition			
Year	Number of Strikes		Men Involved
1934	1,856		1,466,695
1935	2,014		1,117,213
1936	2,172		788,648
1937	4,740		1,890,621
Total	10,782	Total	5,233,627
Average Per Year	2,695.5	Average Per Year	1,308,294

—Monthly Labor Review; May, 1939; p. 1112

During the four years following prohibition, the average number of strikes per year shot up to more than double the average during the thirteen dry years, and more than double as many men were involved. (See page 31)

That result was inevitable. Drink takes the drinker's money and makes him less dependable, hence less efficient, reliable and productive. As a consequence, he gets no increases in pay or promotions. Therefore he feels the pinch of poverty since he wastes his wages to buy his drinks. Hence he cannot properly care for his family. This naturally increases poverty and labor troubles, with more suffering, more loss of time, more economic loss to labor and to the nation.

LIFE INSURANCE

With repeal came a precipitate slump in the amount of new life insurance written. The highest written during any year of prohibition was more than four and a half billion dollars greater than the highest amount written during repeal.

Figures are available for only five years since repeal, during which time the average amount of new life insurance written has dropped to $9,483,891,000 per year or a loss of over a billion and a half per year in the amount of new protection of the American family.

NEW LIFE INSURANCE WRITTEN IN U.S.A. For the First Five Years After the Repeal of Prohibition

1933 - - - - - - - - - - - -	$ 9,113,959,258
1934 - - - - - - - - - - - -	9,395,207,858
1935 - - - - - - - - - - - -	9,416,743,140
1936 - - - - - - - - - - - -	9,481,147,558
1937 - - - - - - - - - - - -	10,012,397,825
Average Per year - - - - -	9,483,891,200

(For comparison with prohibition years, see page 35)

Q. Did repeal sharply affect the average per capita income?

A. That question would almost answer itself. It is well-known that the hard drinker produces less than the same person would if he did not drink. Science steps in and points out that even the very moderate drinker is measurably affected in all of the finer and more delicate tasks. One drink containing as much as one-half ounce of absolute alcohol (a glass of beer, wine or spirits of usual strength) measurably affects fine and delicate operations and coordinations. Students of the question know that very moderate habitual use of alcohol interferes with the reliability, efficiency and ambition of the drinker. Everybody knows that excessive use impairs or even wholly destroys the usefulness of the user. This much is certain: The record clearly shows that the average per capita income was much less before prohibition, and less since repeal than during the time the Eighteenth Amendment was in effect.

The last ten years before prohibition the average per capita income, including men, women and children, was $387.30 per year. During prohibition the average climbed to $575.46, or an increase of 48.5 per cent. For the six years since repeal the per capita income dropped to $454.50. (Report of National Industrial Conference Board, p. 7)

(For comparison with prohibition and pre-prohibition years, see page 34)

TAXES

Q. How much does the liquor traffic pay to the federal, state, and local governments in taxes? A. First, let us keep in mind that the consumer always pays the revenue. To lose sight of that fact at any time leads to inaccurate conclusions.

To illustrate, suppose the state puts a tax of 3c per gallon on gasoline. Who pays that tax? To ask that question is really to answer it; everybody knows that the consumer, the man who buys the gasoline, pays the tax. True, he does not pay it to the state; he pays it to the attendant—at the gasoline station, who in turn pays it to the distributor, and so on, until it reaches the state treasurer. But the point is the user pays the tax. When a man buys an imported hat or an imported watch it is the consumer who pays the tax. The same thing is true when a man buys a schooner of beer, or a shot of whiskey, or a beaker of wine. The consumer pays.

The brewer, distiller and saloon keeper boast loudly about the taxes they pay to the governments. But what they really do, and all they do, to support the government is to collect money from the drinker and hand over to the government its percentage of what the drinkers pay them. They are tax collectors who get rich at the job, while, by the aid of "habit" or diseased craving, they rob their customers of money and also of ability to earn money. All of the millions that the liquor traffic pays the local, state and federal governments come from the pockets of the men and women, and the boys and girls who drink.

Political science teaches, with finality, that while the liquor seller robs the drinker of money, since he gives no value for it, alcohol robs the drinker of some portion of his mental ability, of his acquired skill, and his moral character. This greatly increases the number of people who have become a burden on society through crime, accidents, disease and inefficiency; it adds greatly to the number of broken homes, pauperized children, and to general social degradation.

Q. What about the great reduction in taxes that was promised by the rcpealists?

A. That was a good—though serious—joke! Taxes have steadily increased in spite of the money paid by the drinkers through the brewers, distillers, saloons, night clubs and joints.

In 1932, the Association Against the Prohibition Amendment stated that the annual Federal revenue from beer alone would be over a billion dollars and some silly wets estimated as high as five billion dollars; but by careful computation from the records the Distilled Spirits Institute finds that the total paid in 1938 in revenue taxes, import duties, alcohol beverage control revenues, sales, public and property taxes of varied character to federal, state and municipal governments aggregated $947,277,086.93. (V August, 1940). But it must not be forgotten that this was not paid by the breweries, distilleries and wineries, but by the drinkers.

In 1932, the last year before the repeal of prohibition the national debt was 19 billion dollars, most of it accumulated as the result of the World War. After seven years of repeal the debt had mounted to more than 40 billions and is rocketing to new stratospheric altitudes. We were promised that repeal would lower taxes, balance the budget, and reduce the national debt. But under repeal taxes have shot up above the clouds, the budget has forgotten the meaning of "balance" and the national debt has passed the safety limit set by experts and is still mounting giddily.

Q. What about the actual consumption of alcoholic liquors since repeal?

A. Perhaps it would be wise to refresh our memories concerning the history just preceding the adoption of prohibiiton. The great drive for state and local prohibition really got under way in 1910, which would be ten years prior to the adoption of national constitutional prohibition. In 1910, there were eight dry states; in the next twenty years 20 states went dry; and along with that, large areas went dry under local and county option. In 1910 the consumption of alcoholic liquor according to the U. S. Government was 2,045,353,450 gallons, or 21.84 gallons per capita. (SA 1922; p. 697).

By 1919, the year before national prohibition, at which time there were 33 dry states, the consumption was only 9.28 gallons per capita. (SA. 1922). In 1920, under prohibition it had dropped down to 2.84. This was the lowest in the recorded history of the United States.

It is freely admitted that there was much bootleg liquor. Probably all careful students of the question will admit, however, that there was probably as much bootleg liquor manufactured and drunk during license days as there was after. The reason for this is that under license bootlegging is fairly safe because where legal sale abounds it is very difficult to prove that any liquor found in the possession of a suspect has not been secured legally; whereas, during prohibition if a man was found with liquor, that in itself was a crime unless the possessor could prove his right to it. Hence bootlegging was much more dangerous.

Joseph H. Choate, Jr., who was the director of the

Federal Alcohol Control Administration, said in the January, 1935, Red Book, that half of the spirits consumed in the United States was from illegal sources. He would know. And if he is right, there is unquestionably much more bootlegging since repeal than before. This idea was corroborated by the "Washington Star" of April 29, 1934, which said editorially:

> "The bootlegger and his criminal allies have made the pleasant discovery that wonders never cease, and that there is as much gold at the end of the repeal rainbow as they ever found during the halcyon days of prohibition."

Now going back to the figures and graph on page seven which show that in 1920 the consumption of alcohol had dropped to 2.84. Of course, to this there must be added the bootleg and moonshine consumption. In an attempt to determine how much bootleg and moonshine there was the government made an estimate of 7.12 gallons per capita, as shown on the graph. It is probable that there was not much more, if any, bootlegging during prohibition than before or since. This observation seems to be fully supported by such statements as that of Mr. Choate and the Washington Star quoted above.

With the graph still before us, the irregular light line which runs up to 8.96 gallons in 1930 is the estimate of the amount of bootleg and moonshine made under prohibition as estimated by the compiler of the wet handbook, *The New Crusade.*

Now consulting the graph once more, the consumption of legal liquor for 1940 had climbed to 13.78 gallons. This brings the comparison down on all fours with the earlier years in the graph as the figures in all instances except from 1920 to 1932 when there was no beverage liquor except bootleg. All other years there was legal liquor plus bootleg. The consumption of bootleg can only be estimated, and the light, waving line is a "wild" estimate. Some government authorities have estimated bootleg consumption of spirits to be equal to tax paid.

Q. Has there been an increase in crime, since repeal?

A. Yes. It is thoroughly known the world around that drinking dulls the sensibilities and restraints and increases both vice and crime. Here is a news story three years after repeal:

"Two-thirds of youth crime and juvenile delinquency in Minneapolis can be traced to beer parlors and taverns. As the breeding ground of crime and immorality, beer parlors have taken the place of corner poolrooms from which mothers guarded their sons a generation ago. Beer parlors offer undesirable social contacts which were impossible in the blind pigs of prohibition or the saloons of pre-war days.

"Thousands of dollars are spent annually in the city to apprehend, prosecute and punish or supervise boys and girls who get into trouble from drinking or from undesirable associations in beer parlors.

"Mrs. Blanche Jones, head of the police department women's bureau, reported a sharp increase in the number of minor girls and young women who have come to her attention since repeal of prohibition. County Attorney Ed. J. Goff, stated 70 per cent of the youthful criminals prosecuted by his office admitted that they were intoxicated when they committed crime. Approximately 90 per cent of the illegitimate births in the county result from acquaintances formed in drinking places, according to Assistant County Attorney Lucien Selover. Most girls involved in such cases are between 18 and 22 years old. Frank P. Porestal, superintendent of police, said 70 or 75 per cent of police calls after 11 p.m. are to beer parlors and bars. Many of the fights and disorders involve boys and girls, he said."

(Minneapolis Star, 4-21-39).

Jumping to Chicago:

"Referring to his experience in the Boys' Court of Chicago, Judge J. M. Braude said:

'The surprising thing to me is that boys are under the impression that beer is not intoxicating. When I question a lad about his delinquent acts, I ask him if he had any liquor. His answer invariably is, "No, sir, I just had a couple of beers." They don't seem to realize that beer is intoxicating. About 40 per cent of the boys coming into my court today are beer drinkers. (US, 4-22-39).

J. Edgar Hoover, director of the FBI of the Federal Department of Justice, stated in an address:

"Crime has reached a pinnacle of appalling heights. It lives next door to us. It rubs elbows with us. Its blood-caked hands touch ours. A lackadaisical attitude now has resulted in a crisis.

"No American home is free of its shadow. Aggravated robbery, theft, arson, rape, felonious assault or murder annually is visited upon one of every 16 homes in America. Last year in this supposedly enlightened, advanced, civilized country, there was a minimum of 12,000 murders and an estimated total of 1,445,581 major crimes. Thus one of every 84 persons in the United States was subjected to injury or death through the workings of this tremendous crime aggregate.

"Beyond this there is a constant toll of the rackets; here no home is exempt. The criminal toll is taken upon food and services, and actual physical violence includes the loss of life itself. The American home and every person in it is today in a state of siege The crime problem in America is something which should take precedence before any subject other than that of livelihood itself. Even then it becomes a correlated subject because it is costing each American citizen a minimum of $120 a year. This is the per capita tax which must be assessed to pay our annual crime bill, estimated to be more than $15,000,000,000. If the entire cost of crime could be eliminated for two years, that saving would pay the entire cost of America's share in the World War, plus an enormous bonus."

This amazing figure of 1,445,541 major crime means that there is a major crime committed in the United States each 22 seconds—in other words, almost three major crimes per minute and over 165 major crimes per hour, night and day, holidays and Sundays. Mr. Hoover puts the crime cost of the nation per year at $15,000,000,000 which means that each man, woman and baby in America would pay an average of $120 per year as a crime tax. That is $600 per year, or $50 per month for a family of five.

There is absolutely no student of the question that does not agree that with the increase in the consumption of alcohol there is always an increase in crime because drink breaks down inhibitions, dulls the moral and physical sensibilities and weakens self-control.

THE COURTS

Q. Is there a sound legal basis for prohibiting the manufacture and sale of intoxicating liquors?

A. Yes. Blackstone, the great British authority, says:

"The law is a rule of civil conduct, prescribed by the supreme power of a state, commanding what is right and prohibiting what is wrong."

The British Court of King's Bench, in a decision rendered by Lord Mansfield, said:

"If any pretended principle of law is advanced to prevent the application of the rule of right, the pretended principle is certainly wrong, and cannot require the court to determine that to be true, which the court believes and knows to be untrue."

Q. Have the U.S. Courts spoken on that question?

A. Yes. The Supreme Court of the United States in the case of Crowley vs. Christenson, 137 U. S. 86, said:

"It is urged that, as the liquors are used as a beverage, and the injury following them, if taken in excess, is voluntarily inflicted, and is confined to the party offending, their sale should be without restrictions, the contention being that what a man shall drink, equally with what he shall eat, Is not properly matter for legislation.

"There is in this position an assumption of a fact which does not exist, that when the liquors are taken in excess the injuries are confined to the party offending. The injury, it is true, first, falls upon him in his health, which the habit undermines; in his morals, which it weakens; and in the self-abasement which it creates. But, as it leads to neglect of business and waste of property and general demoralization, it affects those who are immediately connected with and dependent upon him.

"By the general concurrence of opinion of every civilized and Christian community, there are few sources of crime and misery to society equal to the dram shop, where intoxicating liquors, in small quantities, to be drunk at the time, are sold indiscriminately to all parties applying. The statistics of every state show a greater amount of crime and misery attributable to the use of ardent spirits obtained at these retail liquor saloons than to any other source.

"No one possesses an inalienable or constitutional right to keep a saloon for the sale of intoxicating liquor; to keep a saloon for the sale of intoxicating liquor is not a natural right to pursue an ordinary calling; there is no inherent right in a citizen to thus sell intoxicating liquor by retail; it is not a privilege of a citizen of the state or of the United States."

The United States Supreme Court has, in at least twelve different cases, rendered decisions of similar import. The Supreme Courts of many states have joined in the same conclusion.

In the case of Harrison vs. People, 222 Illinois 150, the Supreme Court said:

"It must be conceded that the business of keeping a saloon or dramshop is one which no citizen has a natural or inherent right to pursue."

In State vs. Mississippi, 101 U. S. 814, the United States Supreme Court says:

"No legislature can bargain away the public health or the public morals. The people themselves cannot do it, much less their servants. Government is organized with a view to their preservation, and cannot divest itself of the power to provide for them."

Again, in the case of Mugler vs. Kansas: 123 U. S. 205, the United States Supreme Court said:

"It is not necessary, for the sake of justifying the state legislation, now under consideration, to array the appalling statistics of misery, pauperism, and crime which have their origin in the use or abuse of ardent spirits.

"For we cannot shut out of view the facts, within the knowledge of all, that the public health, the public morals, and the public safety, may be endangered by the general use of intoxicating drinks; nor the fact established by statistics accessible to everyone, that the idleness, disorder, pauperism, and crime existing in the country, are, in some degree at least, traceable to this evil."

The Supreme Court of Illinois in Goddard vs. President, 15 111. 589, says:

"It is not sufficient to say that liquors are property, and their sale is as much secured as that of any other property. Their sale for use as a common beverage and tippling is hurtful and injurious to the public morals, good order arid wellbeing of society. When we defend the sale of liquors for the purpose of tippling, we surely draw our arguments from our appetites, and not our reason, observation and experience."

In Haggart vs. Stehlin, 137 Indiana 43, the Supreme Court of that state said:

"No person has a right to carry on, upon his own premises or elsewhere, for his own gain or amusement, any public business clearly calculated to injure and destroy public morals or to disturb the public peace. No man is at liberty to use his own property without reference to the health, comfort or reasonable enjoyment of like public or private rights by others."

The Supreme Court of South Carolina, in the case of the State ex rel George vs. Aiken, 26 L. R. A. 345, said:

"Liquor, in its nature, is dangerous to the morals, good order, health and safety of the people, and is not to be placed upon the same footing with the ordinary commodities of life, such as corn, wheat, cotton, potatoes, etc."

The Supreme Court of Kansas, in the case of Durien vs. State, 80 Pac. 987, said:

"The commodity in controversy is intoxicating liquor. The article is one whose moderate use, even, is taken into account by actuaries of insurance companies, and which bars employment in classes of service involving prudent and careful conduct-—an article conceded to be fraught with such contagious peril to society, that it occupies a different status before the courts and the legislatures from other kinds of property, and places traffic in it upon a different plane from other kinds, of business. It is still the prolific source of disease, misery, pauperism, vice and crime."

Judge Gookins, in the case of Beebe vs. the State, 6 Ind. 542, said:

"That drunkenness is an evil, both to the individual and to the state, will probably be admitted. That its legitimate consequences are disease and destruction to the mind and body will also be granted. That it produces from four-fifths to nine-tenths of all the crimes committed, is the united testimony of those judges, prison-keepers, sheriffs, and others engaged in the administration of the criminal law, who have investigated the subject. That taxation to meet the expenses of pauperism and crime, falls upon and is borne by the people, follows as a matter of course. That its tendency is to destroy the peace, safety and well-being of the people, to secure which the first article in the Bill of Rights declares all free governments are instituted, is too obvious to be denied."

The City Prosecutor of Chicago recently said:

"It is true that three-fourths of the crimes of Chicago are due to the saloon." (LO. p. 36).

A. F. Knotts, a former Mayor of Hammond, Indiana, said:

"Ninety-five per cent of all crimes is caused directly or indirectly by drink. The police records of our city show that more than ninety per cent of all the offenses committed are the results of intemperance; and that the police force is almost wholly and exclusively employed in watching and caring for men, women and children affected by drink." (LO. p. 36).

Chief Justice Coleridge of the British Court said:

"Nine-tenths of all the criminals that come before the court are made criminals by the saloon. If we could make England sober, we could shut up nine-tenths of her prisons." Is the business that makes nine-tenths of the criminals in England right or wrong? (LO. p. 43).

In Schwouchow vs. Chicago. 68 Illinois 444, the Illinois Supreme Court estimated the saloon as follows:

"We presume no one would have the hardihood to contend that the retail sale of intoxicating drinks does not tend, in a large degree, to demoralize the community, to foster vice, produce crime and beggary, want and misery."

Q. Are there decisions confirming the validity of the 18th Amendment?

A. Yes. Every aspect of that amendment was brought before the U. S. Supreme Court. There were forty or fifty cases involving the validity of the amendment; the method of its adoption; its formal regularity; its division of powers with the states; its relation to other constitutional provisions' most of which were attempts at legalistic technicalities and pettifogging trickery. As an example, it was contended that the power to amend the Constitution was confined solely to subjects covered by the original document and did not extend to amendments that would add new subjects.

The Supreme Court, in passing on the question, set these objections aside as follows:

"That part of the Prohibition Amendment to the Federal Constitution which embodies the prohibition is operative throughout the entire territorial limits of the U. S., binds all legislative bodies, courts, public officers, and individuals within those limits, and of its own force invalidates every legislative act, whether by Congress or by a state legislature, or by a territorial assembly, which authorizes or sanctions what the amendments prohibits."(Rhode Island vs. Palmer, 253 U.S. 350.)

The brewers, distillers, and liquor dealers demanded compensation. But the many judicial decisions, some of which are cited below, denied the claim on the ground that the liquor business is not a right, but it is a privilege granted by law, which privilege might be withdrawn at any time without compensation first because those who enter the liquor business know that the liquor trade is not a natural, inherent or constitutional right. On the other hand it was held, it is a moral, social, and economic evil as is cited above. (Ruppert vs. Caffey, 2S1 U.S. 264, 302; Rhode Island vs. Palmer, 253 U.S. 350; Samuels vs. McCurdy, 267 U.S. 188.)

In the National Prohibition Cases (253 U.S. 350), the court, by Justice Van Devanter, said:

> "While recognizing that there are limits beyond which Congress cannot go in treating beverages as within its power of enforcement, we think those limits are not transcended by the provisions of the Volstead Act. (Title, II, I.) Wherein liquors containing as much as one-half of one per cent of alcohol by volume and fit for use for beverage purposes are treated as within that power."

This much is sure, that in the United States anything that is destructive of "life, liberty and the pursuit of happiness" is outside the pale of the law. Moreover, no social fact is more thoroughly established by history and science than that the traffic in alcoholic beverages is the chief destroyer of these social values.

'Bootleggers operating stills in Cuyahoga county (Ohio) produced sufficient illicit liquor, which found a ready market in the city, to defraud the federal and state governments of more than $200,000 a month in taxes in the fiscal year that ended June, 30." (Cleveland Plain Dealer, 8-6-40).

PHYSIOLOGICAL

Alcohol is a narcotic drug of the chemical family known as hydrocarbons—to which morphine, cocaine and heroin belong. These are the chief narcotics which are classified as habit-forming drugs. Alcohol is the most dangerous morally, socially and economically because it is the most widely and generally used. Ethyl alcohol (used as beverage) is derived from fermentation of sugar.

The drug falls in three general classes: malt liquors—beer, stout, porter, etc.; fermented liquors, such as wines, cider and other fruit juices, which are the result of the direct fermentation of the sugar in fruits; and distilled liquors, which are produced by distilling the alcohol out of either the malt liquors or the fermented fruit juices. Whiskey is distilled from fermented grains; brandies from fermented fruits, rum from fermented sugar, etc.

Beer, as it is sold on the market, contains from 2.75 to 8% alcohol by volume. Wines contain from 8 to 20 per cent alcohol by volume; distilled liquors are concentrated to "proof", which means 50 per cent by volume. However, before spirits are put on the retail market, they are generally "cut" or "blended" to about 35 or 40 per cent alcohol content.

Q. Is there not some minimum amount of alcohol that could be taken without any Injurious effect?

A. Possibly. The late Dr. Emil Kraepelin, the noted German scientist, a moderate beer drinker as most Germans are, spent years in careful experimenting in the universities of Germany where he was able to impose laboratory conditions upon his subjects. This was his conclusion:

"The powers of conception and judgment are from the beginning distinctly affected, although he who takes the alcohol is quite unconscious that it has this effect. The actual facts are exactly the opposite to the popular belief. I must confess that my own experiments, extending over more than ten years, and the theoretical deductions therefrom, have made me an opponent of alcohol." (A3 p. 80.)

Therefore he became a total abstainer. The late Dr. Matthael, staff physician in the German Army, said: ,

"We should not discuss moderation with a man. The thing has long since been settled by science. The use of narcotic poisons is simply indecent and criminal." (M. 122-29).

The late Dr. Sir Victor Horsley: (EB)

"In reality we have no proof that a minimum and permissible dose of alcohol exists." (M. 12-2-29.)

Dr. Robert Koppa:

"The abuse of alcohol commences with its use." (M. 122-29.)

Dr. Metchnikoff: (EB)

"When you take alcohol, you poison the cells of your body." (M. 12-2-29.)

Dr. Haven Emerson (WW) says:

"Alcohol is a depressant habit forming narcotic drug.

"Alcohol is a protoplasmic poison.

"Alcohol is drunk to get the drug effect and whenever it is so taken in whatever amount it exerts to some degree its depressant and toxic effects."

In the minds of a great many honest people, beer is an innocent, at least comparatively innocent, member of the alcohol family. They believe that beer is harmless because a man may drink several glasses and still be able to walk straight and talk straight and perform the ordinary acts of life without any indication that he is abnormal.

It is very generally recognized among medical authorities that a steady, moderate drinker of beer suffers greater health impairment than the steady moderate drinker of spirits. The beer drinker gets fat and flaccid and succumbs quickly to serious and often to trivial disorders. Dr. Gustav von Bunge the noted scientist, physician and professor of physiology in the University of Basel, Switzerland, said in his well known treatise, "The Alcohol Question:"

"Beer is the most harmful of alcoholic drinks."

Dr. Sir William Osier, (EB) formerly of the University of Pennsylvania and Johns Hopkins and later of Oxford, England, expressed similar sentiment in his speech at Working Men's College in 1906.

A body of statistics covering a large field indicates that the beer habit is a harder habit to break than either the wine or the spirit habit. In depressions when most must cut off their luxuries, consumption of spirits and wine decline much more quickly than beer. Moreover, beer recovers from the depression much more quickly than either wine or spirits. Some students hold that beer gets a more tenacious hold on its victims, because of the drug lupulin, which is present in beer and derived from hops.

In the United States, prior to prohibition, beer represented about 90 per cent of the volume of the liquor traffic, wine and spirits representing together only about 10 per cent. In 1914 the per capita consumption of beer in the U. S. was 20.60 gallons, of wine, 53 gallons, and of whiskey 1.44 gallons. (SA 1922—p. 697.) v

Q. Is 8.2 per cent (by weight) beer Intoxicating?

A. Yes. The late Harvey W. Wiley (EB), one of the best known chemists of his time, said under oath:

"Beer containing 2.75 per cent alcohol by weight has a sufficient amount of alcohol to intoxicate the average person in quantities often consumed." (H4 p. 21.)

Abel R. Todd, official chemist for the state of Michigan, under oath, states that:

"Beer containing 3 per cent by volume is intoxicating." (H4 p. 24.)

Dr. Arthur Dean Bevan (WW) former president of the American Medical Association, states under oath:

"There can be absolutely no doubt but that beer containing 2.75 per cent alcohol is an intoxicating beverage and that an individual can become drunk on the amount that is frequently consumed." (H4 p. 25.)

(Much additional evidence will be found in H4).

Q. How much alcohol is required to intoxicate a person?

A. Intoxication begins as soon as any appreciable quantity of an intoxicant is taken into the circulation. Dr. Walter L. Miles (WW) of Yale University, who is said to have made the most exhaustive modern study of this question, states:

"Toxic state means modified nerve condition and action, the result of some poisonous chemical agent. It is exhibited both physiologically and psychologically. Mild toxic changes may be interesting or pleasant to the person having them.

"The range of the psychological effects from ingested alcohol is wide, varying from the slightest change of subjective feeling to complete stupor and utter incapacity known as deep narcosis. * * *

"In the usual parties where alcoholic beverages are taken with food, I have tried to arrange in the form of a scale of the basis of this, you might call, I suppose, 'A scale of toxic symptoms for alcohol.'"

Alcohol in the blood mg. per cc.

1. 0.10 Clearing of the head. Mild tingling of the mucous membrane of the mouth and throat.

2. 0.20 Slight fullness and mild throbbing at back of head. Touch of dizziness. Sense of warmth and general physical well-being. Small bodily aches and fatigue relieved. Feeling tone of pleasantness.

3. 0.30 Mild euphoria. "Everything is all right," "very glad I came," etc. No sense of worry. Feelings of playing a very superior game. Time passes quickly.

4. 0.40 Lots of energy for the things he wants to do. Talks much and rather loudly, hands tremble slightly, movements a bit clumsy; unembarrassed; makes glib or flippant remarks. Memories appear rich and vivid.

5. 0.50 Sitting on top of the world. Normal inhibitions practically cut off, takes personal social liberties

of all sorts as impulse prompts. Enlarges on his past ex-
ploits. "Can lick anybody in the country." Marked blunt-
ing of self-criticism.

6. 0.70 Rapid strong pulse and breathing. Amused at
his own clumsiness or rather at what he takes to be the
perversity of things about him.

7. 1.00 Staggers very perceptibly. Talks to himself.
Fumbles long with the keys in unlocking and starting his
car. Feels drowsy, sings loudly, complains that others
don't keep on their side of the road.

8. 2.00 Needs help to walk or to undress. Easily an-
gered. Shouts, groans, and weeps by turns. Is nauseat-
ed and has poor control of urination. Cannot recall with
whom he spent the evening.

9. 3.00 In a stuporous condition, very heavy breathing, sleeping and vomiting by turns. No comprehension
of language.

10. 4.00 Deep anesthesia, may be fatal. (H4. pp. 514-
5)

Q. How much 2.75 per cent (by weight) beer would
one have to drink to be visibly intoxicated?

A. About 1 and three quarters to 2 pints, according to Dr. Miles, would perceptibly affect motions, and
slow down action noticeably. This would be the condition at .30 on the scale. It would be produced by about
three-quarters of an ounce of absolute alcohol. (H4. p.
519.)

Q. How much would one drink to be drunk enough to
attract the attention of the police?

A. Dr. Miles states that it would require about 4 pints of 2.75 per cent beer. (H4. p. 520.) This would be the condition indicated at 1.00 on the chart. This would be about one and onefourth ounces of absolute alcohol.

Q. Does the ordinary glass of whiskey contain much more alcohol than the ordinary glass of beer?

A. No. There is not much difference between the actual content of absolute alcohol in the various dilutions that make the usual alcoholic drinks as we know them. A 12 ounce bottle of 4 per cent beer contains .48 ounce of absolute alcohol. An ounce and a half of proof whiskey contains .75 ounce absolute alcohol. But whiskey is generally sold in blended form containing from 30 per cent to 40 per cent, an ounce and a half of which would carry .45 to .60 ounce of alcohol. A three ounce glass of light 10 per cent wine would carry .30 ounce of absolute alcohol. Three ounces of 20 per cent wine would carry twice as much, or .60 ounce. A highball containing 1.2 oz. of 40 per cent whiskey and a 12 oz. glass of 4 per cent beer would contain identically the same amount of alcohol.

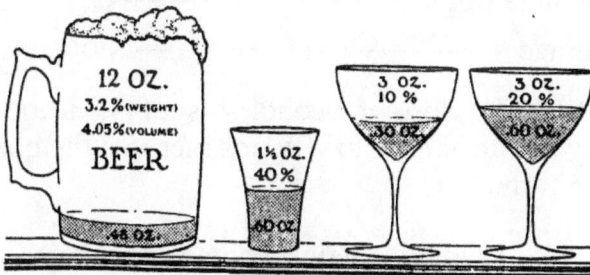

Q. Would one or two highballs or one or two glasses of beer make a man drunk?

A. These amounts would probably not make the average adult stagger or stutter or show any visible sign of intoxication. It might make him "lively". Scientific tests establish the fact that his finer perceptions and reactions are retarded,

The Minneapolis Journal, when beer was first legalized, printed this list of pre-prohibition beers, showing that four of them were stronger and six weaker than 3.2% now called nonintoxicating.

Brand

Blatz, Wiener	3.7
Eidelweiss	3.3
Schlitz, Pale	3.15
Babst, Blue Ribbon	2.9
Budweiser	3.8
Bohemian	2.5
Huating Weiss Bier	2.6
Graff Weiss Beer	2.8
Jung Pilsener	2.8
Old Style Lager	3.4
Average	3.09

Q. Would a dose of alcohol so small as to be unnoticed by the drinker or his friends increase the hazard of modern traffic?

A. Yes. Though many people doubt it, probably the most dangerous driver is one who shows no sign of intoxication and who truthfully insists that he feels no effect of the alcohol he has drunk. Many scientific studies have reached the conclusion that, confronted by an emergency, the average normal driver takes one-fifth of a second to react—i.e., to apply the brake, swing the steering gear, etc. "Experiments of the Research Committee have shown that this 'reaction time' as medical men term it, is doubled or trebled by a dose of alcohol equal to that in two ounces of whiskey." (A4 p. 27)

Q. Would it be as dangerous for a driver to drink a pint bottle of beer?

A. No. But it would be dangerous. A pint of 3.2 per cent beer carries .64 oz. of absolute alcohol, while 2 oz. of whiskey would carry .70 to .80 oz-. Two ounces of "proof" whiskey, which is not usually sold except on physician's prescription would carry 1 oz. absolute alcohol. Two pint bottles of 3.2 per cent (by weight) beer would carry 1.28 oz. Most men would probably not "feel" a bottle, or perhaps two, of mild beer, or two ounces of 35 per cent or 40 per cent whiskey. A woman was arrested in Minneapolis (April, 1933) for running over a man and killing him. One policeman testified that she was sober, the other that she was slightly intoxicated. She swore she was perfectly sober, having drunk only two cocktails. She was imperfectly sober—not intoxicated enough to "feel" it, yet intoxicated enough to slow her nerve processes down to the degree shown by scientific tests.

Q. Do traffic officers generally recognize these facts, or are they scientific theories?

A. These facts are generally if not universally recognized by highway traffic men. Robbins Stoeckel (WW), professor of Highway Transportation, Yale University, states:

"The really dangerous driver is the man who has had one or two drinks only, who still thinks he is in possession of his faculties, but whose driving judgment is impaired. On the highways moderate drinking is more dangerous than immoderate, and on this account the authorities, in order to protect the public safety must reckon with the effects of moderate drinking." (NE p. 36)

Many other highway men have given expression to the same sentiment.

"Alcohol causing a state of intoxication was a factor in 90 per cent of the traffic deaths occurring here (Cleveland, Ohio) between midnight and 5 a.m., Coroner Samuel R. Gerber reported yesterday in a summary of vehicular fatalities for the first eight months of the year. In the 65 tests made this year of accidents at all hours, 57 per cent of the victims were intoxicated, Dr. Gerber said. This compares with 47 per cent in 1930 dry .... Although the victims' ages ranged from 20 to 75, the heaviest alcohol incidence was found in the 30-to-40 age group." (Cleveland Plain Dealer, 9-6-40).

"In 1910, sixty-one mental cases with alcohol psychoses were admitted to Salem, Oregon, State Hospital .... During sixteen years of state and national prohibition such cases dropped to an all-time low of ten in 1921 and an average of only 20.3 cases annually, as compared to an average of 54.6 cases under the legalized liquor traffic from 1910 to 1914. Prohibition repeal brought an upward leap in the number of alcohol psychoses cases, an all-time high of 102 cases being reached in 1937." (Christian Advocate, published in American Issue, April, 1940.)

HISTORY

The tragedies of intoxicants and intoxication mar the earliest chapters of the history of the race. The teaching of temperance and of total abstinence are also found in very remote records. Total abstinence was adopted by certain priestly and religious orders in ancient times, and the laws of some of the nations restricted the traffic in alcohol and imposed penalties, in some cases to death, for drunkenness, although for the most part drink was considered a good servant. Until very modern times alcohol, in moderation, was believed to be a health and strength building food.

The first voluntary total abstinence society which is fully authenticated by history was "The Union Temperance Society of Moreau and Northumberland" organized near Glen Falls, N.Y. by Dr. Billy Clark in 1808. This voluntary temperance movement spread sporadically.

The centennial of the early temperance organizations formed in Ireland and England were celebrated in 1933.

The first prohibitory law among English speaking people was doubtless the ordinance of the colony of Connecticut which, in 1654, prohibited sale of liquor to Indians (SE. v. 2, p. 687). This was followed by like legislation in most of the colonies. In 1733 the Board of Trustees of the colony of Georgia prohibited the manufacture, sale, or importation of spirituous liquors. One hundred years later, Liberty and Camden Counties in Georgia adopted what was probably the first county prohibition act— the beginning of county option. (SE. v. 3, p. 1077-78)

The first speech of record advocating prohibition in the British House of Parliament was in 1743 when Lord

Chesterfield, one of England's greatest statesmen, spoke against a measure to tax intoxicating liquors. This classic began, "Luxury, my lords, should be taxed, but vice prohibited, let the difficulties in executing the law be what they will." (SE. p. 567, and in many other similar works.)

Q. What other agitation and legislation preceded the adoption of the 18th amendment?

A. As an outgrowth of the Civil War, the United States Brewers Association, which grew to be a tremendously powerful organization, was born. But the temperance forces were also organizing. The Blue Ribbon and the Red Ribbon and other total abstinence organizations flourished; Father Matthew of Ireland and John B. Gough, a reclaimed drunkard and a fervid apostle of temperance, set the nation aflame with temperance enthusiasm. The Independent Order of Good Templars, and the Washingtonians, followed by the Prohibition party in 1869, Women's Christian Temperance Union in 1872 and the National Anti-Saloon League in 1895 all of which, national in their scope of activity, came into being when agitation for temperance and the overthrow of the liquor traffic were at flood.

In the meantime, the popularity of local option had rapidly grown and developed in every part of the nation, and in 1907 a third drive for prohibition by states swept the nation. (PU. Chap. 20.)

Q. How many states banished the legal liquor traffic in this last drive?

A. A total of 30, which with Maine, Kansas, and North Dakota made 33. (See Table, page 88).

Q. Is not the law much more generally and habitually violated under prohibition than under regulation?

A. Under any system the liquor traffic is always habitually lawless. It will be most lawless where it can break the law with the least danger. If it is legal to sell till 10 o'clock it is easy to pull the blinds, and by a side door continue to sell. If it is legal to sell beer it is easy to keep whisky, gin and brandy to be drawn from secret taps. A place protected by law is a base for illegal operation. If it is legal to sell to men and women, one may quite safely sell illegally to boys and girls when the officer's back is turned.

Q. But is it not true that blindpiggers and bootleggers flourish much more under prohibition?

A. No. A bootlegger or blindpigger is fairly safe when there is legal liquor. In Canada voters were urged to abandon prohibition, and adopt government sale to get rid of blindpigs and bootleggers. An official report from the Saskatchewan Liquor Board showed an increase of 111 per cent in bootlegging the first year of government sale. The British Columbia Liquor Board's official report says: "As much liquor is sold by bootleggers as in government stores." Alberta Liquor Board officially reported: "Our greatest problem is moonshine." The Winnipeg Daily Tribune quotes a judge of that city who complains of too many women bootleggers. (Oct. 4, 1928). The Vancouver, British Columbia, local papers referred to that province as a "bootleggers' paradise." Montreal papers carry such headlines as "Curse of Blindpigs in Montreal."

On March 28, 1908, (wet) the Minneapolis papers carried a statement from the Liquor Dealers' Association in which they stated: "Of its own knowledge" that there were 4,000 blindpigs in Minneapolis and Hennepin County. There were at that time 408 licensed saloons. That was one blind pig for each 75 people in the then population. Plain Talk, a wringing wet publication, in its

April, 1930, number, stated that there were in Minneapolis 3.000 speakeasies and beer flats. That was one for
each 150 of population in 1930 (dry). This showed that
there were twice as many blind pigs per population in
1908 under license as in 1930 under prohibition. This is
the testimony of the wets themselves.

Q. Why do not those in the legitimate liquor business
fight against this illegal competition to protect their own
profits?

A. Legitimate liquor business? The legitimate and illegitimate liquor business are usually both in the same
hands. If there is a legitimate liquor business it runs the
"illegitimate" liquor business. No man can get far in the
study of the liquor problem without discovering that in-
disputable fact. The 408 retail liquor dealers in Minneapolis in 1908 did not wish nor dare to make war on the
4,000 blindpigs because the brewers that sold beer to
the 408 saloons also sold beer to the 4,000 blindpigs.
If the saloons fought the blind pigs, they would kill the
brewers, the saloons. If the Minneapolis breweries had
refused to sell to the illegal trade the Milwaukee, St. Louis and Chicago breweries would supply them. Under regulation there is always the legal PLUS the illegal traffic.
John Barleycorn is always lawless.

The Chicago Record Herald of August 19, 1907 (wet)
under a headline

"POLICEMEN DIRECT PATRONS TO BLIND PIG,"
states:

"The Normandy, a hotel, served drinks and provided music in a room just off the hotel office on the
second floor. Entrance was gained through the hotel

entrance. There was a 'copper' stationed at the door to point out the way to strangers. At 2:00 o'clock (in the morning) the little improvised barroom was crowded with men and women in varying stages of intoxication. Male patrons were, for the most part, young men. The women were battered flotsam which the tide of life annually throws into Clark Street from the gaudier haunts of the underworld."

Again the same paper on September 8, 1911, quoted an attorney as follows:

"Conditions in Rogers Park are disgraceful. There are blind pigs everywhere and people in the vicinity have no trouble in buying all the beer and whisky they want. The brewers are behind the blindpig men and fight tooth and nail to have them discharged when arrested."

The breweries openly approved this blindpigging and bootlegging. The Brewers' Journal May 1, 1910, ten years before prohibition, said in an editorial:

"No matter what 'laws' may be made to cripple the beverage industries of our present times, they cannot and will not be observed by those managing these industries."

Q. Did national prohibition come too suddenly, before there had been opportunity to test it out in smaller units, such as villages, counties and states?

A. Hardly. Prohibition had been under test since colonial times, (pages 3-7) and its slow growth indicated that it was undergoing a long and severe try-out. State-wide prohibition had been in force in Maine for 70 years when the 18th Amendment to the Federal Constitution was adopted; Kansas had been dry under her dry constitution for 40 years, and North Dakota for 31, and a total of 33 of the 48 states, and the District of Columbia were dry when National Prohibition came. Here is the record:

TABLE SHOWING THE ORDER IN WHICH STATES ADOPTED STATE-WIDE PROHD3ITION, AND THE DATE WHEN, AND METHOD BY WHICH IT WAS ADOPTED, TOGETHER WITH THE VOTE, AND THE MAJORITY FOR PROHBITION

No. Dry	State	Year	Vote For	Vote Against	Majority For
1	Maine	1851 S			
2	Kansas	1880 C	93,302	84,304	7,998
	Maine	1884 C	70,783	23,811	46,972
3	North Dakota	1889 C	18,552	17,393	1,159
4	Georgia	1907 S			
5	Oklahoma	1907 C	130,361	112,258	18,103
6	Mississippi	1908 S			
7	North Carolina	1908 SR	113,612	69,416	44,196
8	Tennesee	1909 S			
9	West Virginia	1912 C	160,945	72,603	92,342
10	Virginia	1914 SR	94,251	63,886	30,365
11	Oregon	1914 C	136,842	100,362	36,480
12	Washington	1914 SR	189,840	171,208	18,632
13	Calorado	1914 C	129,589	118,017	11,572
14	Arizona	1914 C	25,887	22,743	3,144
15	Alabama	1915 S			
16	Arkansas	1915 S			
17	Iowa	1915 S			
18	Idaho	1915 S			

19	South Carolina	1915 SR	41,735	16,809	24,926
	Idaho	1916 C	90,576	35,456	55,120
20	Montana	1916 C	102,776	73,890	28,886
21	South Dakota	1916 C	65,334	53,360	11,974
22	Michagan	1916 C	353,378	284754	68,624
23	Nebraska	1916 C	146,574	117132	29,442
24	Indiana	1917 S			
25	Utah	1917 S			
26	New Hamp-shire	1917 S			
27	New Mexico	1917 C	28,732	12,147	16,585
	Utah	1918 C	42,691	15,780	26,911
28	Texas	1918 S			
29	Ohio	1918 C	463,654	437,895	25,759
30	Wyoming	1918 C	31,439	10,200	21,239
31	Florida	1918 C	21,851	13,609	8,242
32	Nevada	1918 SR	13,248	9,060	4,188
	Texas	1919 C	159,723	140,099	19,624
33	Kentucky	1919 C	208,905	198,671	10,234

S is for Statutory

SR Statutory by referendum

C is for Constitutional

KEY TO REFERENCES

A American Issue, Westerville, Ohio.

AL Abraham Lincoln—Life and Works—Whitney.

AAPA Association against the Prohibition Amendment

AS Amazing: Story of RepealDobyns-Willett, Clark & Co., Chicago, Hl.

A2 Anti-Saloon League Year Book, Westerville, Ohio.

A3 Alcohol and the Human Body—McMillan Co., New York.

A4 Alcohol British Medical Research Council.

C Christian Science Monitor, Boston.

CI Cyclopedia of Temperance and Prohibition, Punk and Wagnalls, New York.

EB Encyclopedia Britannica, 14th Edition.

E2 Early Speeches of Lincoln. O Great Destroyer—Dr. J. H. Kellogg, Battle Creek.

H Hand Book of Modern Facts About Alcohol, Westerville, Ohio.

H2 Hearings Senate Judicial Committee, 1930; Government Document.

H3 How to Live—Lyman Pisk.

H4 Hearings Ways and Means Committee; 72nd Congress.

LO Legalized Outlaw—S. R. Artman.

References 125

L2 Lobby Investigations; 71st Congress.

M Methodist Clipsheet, Methodist Building, Washington, D. C.

MT Measuring the Liquor Tide.

NE Noble Experiment—Irving Fisher, Hartford, Conn.

NV National Voice, Los Angeles, Calif.

N2 New Crusade, Wet Hand Book.

PP Prohibition and Prosperity—Samuel Crowther.

PU Prohibition in the United States, Colvin—Doran & Co., New York.

PW Prohibition at its Worst—Irving Fisher, Hartford, Conn.

P5 Does Prohibition Work?

SA Statistical Abstract of the United States, Washington, D. C.

SE Standard Encyclopedia of the Liquor Problem, Anti-Saloon League, Westerville, Ohio.

US United States News, Washington, D. C.

V The Methodist Voice, Methodist Building, Washington, D.C.

WA World Almanac, 1940.

WC Wickersham Committee, Report of Washington, D. C. 35,000 Miles of Prohibition—Gordon

BIOGRAPHY

EB: following a name indicates that additional biographical information will be found in the Encyclopedia Britannica, 14th edition.

WW: indicates that a biographical sketch will be found in "Who's Who in America," 1940-1 edition.

SE: indicates that a biographical sketch will be found in the Standard Encyclopedia of the Alcohol Problem, 1925.

ADDAMS, Jane. (WW, EB); LLD. Famous for the establishment of Hull House of Chicago, a world renowned social settlement, President Women's League for Peace and other social betterment organizations. Awarded gold medal of military merit. Author Democracy and Social Ethics; New Ideas of Peace; Spirited Youth and the City Streets; and many other books on social problems, and contributor to magazines and news press.

BEVAN, Arthur D. (WW) A.M., M.D., Fellow of American Surgical Association, Director Surgical Division TJ. S. Surgeon General's Office, Washington, D. C. Officer Legion of Honor France. Author of textbooks on Surgery and Anatomy and Contributor to Medical Magazines.

BOOTH, Evangeline, (EB, WW); Gen. Sal. Army, 30 years Commander-in-chief of U. S. forces of Sal. Army. Hon. M.A.; Awarded D.S.M. (U.S.) for work in World War; Gold medal for eminent patriotic service.; Gold medal Swedish Order of Vassa '33; Gold medal Nat. Inst. Soc. Sciences for services to humanity '33. Author; contributor on religious and social welfare topics.

CHOATE, Jos. H. Jr., (WW); A.B.; LL.B.; Member New York bar; Gov. New York Hosp.; one of founders Chem. Foundation; Chmn. Federal Alcohol Control Administration 1933-1936. CBABTBEE, James William (WW); B.S.; B.A.; M.A.; Sec. Natl. Ed, Assn; State Supt. Pub. Instruction, Neb.; Pres. Wis. Teachers" Col., etc. Many other educ. activities.

CBOWTHER, Samuel. (WW, EB) B.S., LL.B.; Magazine and newspaper correspondent, author of many books and articles on economic, social, industrial and civic questions, including Common Sense and Labor; Why Men Strike; The Book of Business; Prohibition and Prosperity, and others.

DUPONTS. (WW). The DuPont group is the chief owner of E. I. DuPont deNemours and Company, extensive manufacturers in the munition, chemical and allied industries. It is one of the largest manufacturing groups in the United States, and is composed of many corporations. They were the financial leads in the Association Against the Prohibition Amendment which organization was chiefly responsible for repeal.

EMERSON, Haven (WW); A.M.; M.D.; Comm'r. of Health N.Y. City, '15-17; Prof, of Med., etc., Prof. Public Health Adm., Columbia '22—; Col. Med. Corps U.S. Army; Dir. of Health in many cities; decorated by France and U. S. for war service, etc. Author med. works. FARLEY, James A. (WW); Pres. Genl. Bldg. Supply Corp. N.Y. City; Chmn. N.Y. State Dem. Comm.; Chmn. Dem. Natl. Comm., Postmaster General.

FELDMAN, Herman (WW, EB) M.A.; Ph.D.; Prof. Industrial Relations Amos Truck School; Prof. Administration and Finance, Dartmouth College; Dean School of Business and Civic Administration, College of City of New York, etc.; Author and contributor to scientific and economic periodicals.

HOOVER, Herbert Clark. (WW, EB). Thirty-first President of the United States; mining engineer; relief administrator in European countries at the beginning of the World War, afterwards food administrator in the U.S.A.

HOOVER, J. Edgar (WW); LL.D.; Chief of Federal Bureau of Investigation. Awarded "Distinguished Service Medal" by Boys Clubs of America; gold medal for "Distinguished service to humanity" by National Institute of Social Sciences; "Medal of Achievement" by Penn Athletic Club; "Distinguished Service" medal by National Institute of Social Sciences, and others, in U. S. and abroad.

HORSLEY, Sir Victor, (1857-1916) (EB); M.D.; Physiologist and Surgeon, Head London Hosp., etc. Prof. Path. U of London '86; Author.

KIRCHWEY, George W. (WW) A.M., LL.D., former commissioner of prison reform in the State of New York; Warden of Sing Sing, Head of the Department of Criminology in universities; President of American Institute of Criminal Law; President Welfare League of New York, Editor of the Department of Law, of the International Encyclopedia, Author and Contributor on criminal law.

KRAEPELIN, Emil, (1856-1926) (SE) Psychiatrist; M.D.; Prof, in sev. largest European coll. Author of many famous experiments muscular and nervous reactions. Voluminous writer.

MECHNIKOV, Rya, (1845-1916) (EB) Russian biologist; Prof. Zoology and Anatomy, U. of Odessa; co-laborer with Pasteur in Paris; author med. works on microbes and bacteria, etc. Winner Nobel Prize '08.

MILES, Walter Richard, (WW); Psychologist; B.S.; A.B.; M.A., Ph.D.; Prof, and lecturer in several colleges and Univ.'s. etc. Now Prof. Psychiatry Yale. Author numerous books and papers on psychiatry. OSLER, Sir William, (1849-1919) (EB) M.D.; Prof, of Med. in McGill U., U. of Penn., Johns Hopkins, etc.'; Regius Prof, of Med. at Oxford, Eng. Author med. works.

PEABODY, Mrs. Henry W. Social Welfare and missions leader; Secretary and Editor of the Women's Baptist Foreign Missionary Society. Director of the Women's Christian College, Madras; Women's Christian Medical College, Velore, India; Chairman of the Women's National Law Enforcement Committee, etc.; Author and Editor.

ROOSEVELT, Franklin D., (WW) A.B.; LL.D.; Asst. Sec. of the Navy, Governor New York two terms. Elected President of U. S. in 1932, 1936 and 1940. Author numerous books on political questions.

ROOSEVELT, Theodore, (1858-1919) (EB); Ranchman, Col. Rough Riders, Spanish-American war; Governor N.Y.; Vice President and President of the U. S.; leader of Progressive party, 1912. Fearless and colorful world leader.

STOECKEL, Bobbins B. (WW); Hon. MA. Yale; LL.D.; Prof. Highway Transportation Yale U.; Member Conn. State Senate '17; Dir. Hartley-Salmon Clinic; member Conn. State Park and Forest Comm. and Conn. State Police Comm. etc.

TABER, Louis John (WW) Master of the National Grange, Director of the National Live Stock Association; Trustee of the Ohio Agricultural Experiment Association; Member of the Ohio State Library Board; Member of the National Committees of Boy Scouts and 4-H Clubs.

WICKERSHAM, George W. Appointed by President Hoover as Chairman of "The National Commission on Law Observance and Enforcement." This Commission devoted one volume of its five volume report to the enforcement of prohibition.

WILLEBRANDT, Mabel Walker; (WW) LL.D.; served three years as public defender in Los Angeles. Assistant Attorney General of the U.S., in charge of cases arising from federal tax and prohibition laws.

WOODCOCK, Amos W. W., (WW); M.A.; LL.D.; Lieutenant Colonel of the 115th Inf. A.E.F.; cited and promoted for "Gallantry in Action"; Brigadier-General, Md. N.G.; Director of the United States Bureau of Prohibition, 1930-33.

Lincoln on Prohibition

"Whether or not the world would be vastly benefited by a total and final banishment from it of all Intoxicating drinks seems to me not now an open question. Three-fourths of mankind confess the affirmative with their tongues, and I believe all the rest acknowledge it in their hearts * * *

"In it we shall find a stronger bondage broken, a viler slavery manumitted, a greater tyrant deposed; in it, more of want supplied, more of disease healed; more of sorrow assuaged. By it, no orphans starving, no widows weeping. By it none wounded hi feeling, none injured In interest. * * * *

"If the relative grandeur of revolutions shall be estimated by the great amount of human misery they alleviate and the small amount they inflict, then indeed will this be the grandest the world shall ever have seen. * * * *

"And when the victory shall be complete—when there shall be neither a slave nor a drunkard on the earth—how proud the title of that land which may truly claim to be the birthplace of both those revolutions that shall have ended in that victory. How nobly distinguished that people who shall have planted and nurtured to maturity both the political and moral freedom of their species."

Washington's Birthday Speech, delivered before the Washingtonian Temperance Society, in Springfield, Illinois, February 22, 1842.

Recommended Readings

Abbott, Kathryn A. "Alcohol and the Anishinaabeg of Minnesota in the Early Twentieth Century". *The Western Historical Quarterly* 30. no. 1 (1999): 25-43.

Abbott, Kathryn A. "Liquor law in Minnesota Indian country in the early twentieth century". *Legal Studies Forum* 25, no. 3/4 (January 2, 2001): 567-585. *OmniFile Full Text Select (H.W. Wilson)*. EBSCO*host*

American Prohibition Yearbook 1915. Ed. John A. Shields. Chicago: Prohibition National Committee, 1915.

American Prohibition Yearbook 1916. Ed. John A. Shields. Chicago: Prohibition National Committee, 1916.

Andersen, Lisa. "From Unpopular to Excluded: Prohibitionists and the Ascendancy of a Democratic-Republican System, 1888–1912". *Journal of Policy History* 24. no. 2 (2012): 288-318. https://muse.jhu.edu/

Anderson, Lisa M. The Politics of Prohibition: American Governance and the Prohibition Party. New York: Cambridge University Press, 2013.

Calderwood, W.G. A. Lincoln: Reformer: Born February 9, 1809. Minneapolis: Cole and Christianson Co. Publishers, 1909.

Calderwood, W.G. "Prohibition as a Present Political Platform", *The Annals of the American Academy of Political and Social Science* 32 (1908): 106-11

Calderwood, W.G. *Prohibition Facts: Questions and Answers*. Minneapolis: Prohibition Facts Service, 1932.

Calderwood, W.G. *Prohibition Facts: Questions and Answers*. Minneapolis: Prohibition Facts Service, 1933.

Calderwood, W.G. *Prohibition Facts: Questions and Answers*. Minneapolis: Prohibition Facts Service, 1935.

Hill, John Wesley. *Twin City Methodism: Being a History of the Methodist Episcopal Church in Minneapolis and St. Paul Minn..* Ed. Minneapolis: Price Bros. Publishing Co., 1895.

Hudson, Horace B. *A Half Century of Minneapolis*. Minneapolis: The Hudson Publishing Company, 1908.

McGerr, Michael. A Fierce Discontent: The Rise and Fall of the Progressive Movement in America, 1870-1920, Oxford: Oxford University Press, 2005.

Who's who in America, Volume 9. Ed. John William Leonard and Albert Nelson Marquis. Chicago: A. N. Marquis and Company, 1916.

Partisan Prophets, Roger Storms; National Prohibition Foundation Inc., 1972